POWER
Prayers
for
Your Life

BARBOUR
PUBLISHING

Print ISBN 978-1-62416-260-2

eBook Editions:
Adobe Digital Edition (.epub) 978-1-62416-439-2
Kindle and MobiPocket Edition (.prc) 978-1-62416-438-5

Published by Barbour Publishing, Inc., P.O. Box 719, Uhrichsville, Ohio 44683, www.barbourbooks.com

Our mission is to publish and distribute inspirational products offering exceptional value and biblical encouragement to the masses.

Member of the
Evangelical Christian
Publishers Association

Printed in China.

Contents

INTRODUCTION

What does prayer mean to you? At the very heart of the matter, prayer is sharing with God. It opens up a line of communication that links children to Father, creation to Creator, saved to Savior. Sounds pretty simple, right?

But the truth is that many of us (even longtime Christians) struggle to pray. Whether it's because of a too-full schedule or a too-hard heart or an insecurity about what to pray, it's a challenge—but a challenge worth meeting head-on!

No matter where you are in your prayer journey, this book is a great place to start. Within these pages, you'll find the encouragement you need to start conversations with God. Each section opens with a short devotional that will prepare your heart for each life topic covered there. Then short prayer starters will get you headed in the right direction and give you some specific areas to start with. Meditate on the accompanying words of scripture and take full advantage of your prayer time, and soon you'll see the blessings that follow a life that is covered in prayer—daily growing closer to the heart of the One who puts the power in our prayers!

> *The earnest prayer of a righteous person has*
> *great power and produces wonderful results.*
> JAMES 5:16 NLT

MY ATTITUDE—THE POWER OF MY THOUGHTS

Positive thoughts are one key to a great attitude. Beating yourself up with thoughts that you'll never be good enough, that you don't deserve to be loved, and that you aren't smart enough will ultimately steal your dream—not to mention take the joy out of your life. It's hard to maintain a great attitude when your thinking is negative. But when you believe what God says about you and your circumstances, then you build something beautiful in your heart and mind.

Don't think that positive thinking is enough—it takes faith to rely on God to bring change to your heart and mind. Past experiences have shaped your attitudes and values about the world around you. The apostle Paul challenges us to "not be conformed to this world, but be transformed by the renewing of your mind, that you may prove what is that good and acceptable and perfect will of God" (Romans 12:2 NKJV).

Somewhere along the life-road you've walked, someone has done something to hurt you. Maybe it wasn't even intentional, but you wanted to see them punished for what they did. You most likely wanted to lash out or pay them back. But God's Word clearly tells you to forgive that person. Depending on how hurt you were, you probably needed some time to sort it all out. Your attitude about that person probably stunk for a while.

God's desire is for you to forgive that person—allow that to sink in and change your thoughts, and eventually you can choose to truly forgive them through your trust in God. It could mean thinking more about God's love and your desire to do His will, rather than thinking about what that person did to you.

The Bible is clear on what we should be thinking about.

"Finally, brethren, whatever things are true, whatever things are noble, whatever things are just, whatever things are pure, whatever things are lovely, whatever things are of good report, if there is any virtue and if there is anything praiseworthy—meditate on these things" (Philippians 4:8 NKJV). The truth may be that the person hurt you, but thinking about that situation isn't lovely or a good report.

When you're tempted to think thoughts that contradict who you are in Christ, counteract them with thoughts about how important you are to God. Take the time to pray and ask God to encourage you. Spending time with Him and thinking about how much He loves you can turn your attitude around. Recount to the Lord all the wonderful things He's done for you. Picture yourself doing the things God put you on the earth to do. Choose your thoughts—change your life!

FOR A MORE POSITIVE ATTITUDE

Lord, You look into my heart and see the truth of how I think and feel. I won't pretend anymore, because I know I can be real with You. Help me to let go of the things that have hurt and angered me. I don't want those things to be my focus. I want to be focused on You and what You have planned for my life today. Help me to do what I need to do without grumbling, complaining, or pointing fingers at others. Fill me with Your joy and strengthen me with Your love.

> *"For the LORD searches all*
> *hearts and understands all*
> *the intent of the thoughts."*
> 1 CHRONICLES 28:9 NKJV

GAINING CONTROL OF MY THOUGHTS

Sometimes I feel like my thoughts are carrying on a conversation and I'm just observing. I feel out of control. But then I remember that You know me better than I know myself. I remember I have control over my thoughts. I turn them toward You and concentrate on what Your Word says about me. I have the mind of Christ. He lived His life saying and doing what You told Him to say and do—and I can, too.

11

TRANSFORMING MY THOUGHTS

Father, Your Word says I can choose what to think about. Help me to refuse thoughts that keep me prisoner to things in my past or to worries about my future. My hope is in You. You are my strength and my shield. Transform my thoughts with the truth of Your Word. When I read the Bible, help me to remember Your Word. Then when my mind wanders to matters that bring me down, I will recall what You have to say about them.

May the words of my mouth and the
meditation of my heart be pleasing to you,
O LORD, my rock and my redeemer.
PSALM 19:14 NLT

CULTIVATING A GOOD ATTITUDE

Lord, the Bible tells me life and death are in the power of the tongue. What comes out of my mouth is first planted in my mind as thoughts. Sometimes I say words I don't mean or later regret. Fill my spirit with Your goodness. Your words are healthy to me. Help me to control what I say by thinking about what pleases You before I open my mouth.

GUARDING MY MIND

Thank You for the helmet of salvation to protect my mind. As I spend time with You and in Your Word, I know I will become more like You. I will guard my mind and refuse to allow negative thoughts to have power over me. Your Word is my weapon to fight the thoughts that oppose who I am in Christ. I will be careful about the things I see and hear because I know they can open my mind to positive or negative thinking. Help me to focus on truth.

You will keep in perfect peace
him whose mind is steadfast,
because he trusts in you.
ISAIAH 26:3

GIVING CONCERNS COMPLETELY TO GOD

When I pray, I give my concerns to You, but later I find that I've made them my responsibility again. Somewhere in my thinking I stop trusting You and try to work problems out on my own. I don't need to know how You are going to resolve them. Forgive me for making problems bigger than You, and show me how to give them completely to You.

AN ATTITUDE OF THANKFULNESS

God, I appreciate the good things You put in my life. I know I take them for granted sometimes, and I don't mean to be that way. I get caught up in the fast-paced busyness of all the things I have to do. I need to remember the simple things that bring me joy: a moment of laughter, a smile from a stranger, and those moments when things are actually going right. I appreciate Your kindness and the fact that You made me Your child. Thank You!

TO BE MORE CONSIDERATE

I could be more considerate. I admit it—I'm usually thinking of myself instead of someone else. Help me to be more considerate of others. Help me to listen when someone is speaking to me. Show me what You want me to say when someone gives me the opportunity to speak to them.

TURNING OBSTACLES INTO OPPORTUNITIES

Lord, You know I can get upset when things don't go my way. I think a situation should play out a certain way, and when it doesn't, I lose focus and let it ruin my whole day. Help me to see obstacles as opportunities to maintain my composure. I want to learn to rise above circumstances. Remind me that in the light of eternity a few moments of inconvenience are not worth the effort and energy I waste in negative emotional responses. Give me wisdom to see life from Your perspective—sometimes my way isn't the best way.

AN ATTITUDE OF HUMILITY

Lord, without You I am nothing. Sometimes I want to rely on myself and do things my own way, but I can't depend on my own morality and virtue. I need Your mercy and grace to become all You created me to be. Help me to be content to be myself. Remind me that I am as good as anyone else, but not better than anyone else. You love equally—You love us all very much!

A TEACHABLE ATTITUDE

Holy Spirit, I invite You to be my teacher, to lead and guide me in all truth. Show me how to let go of selfish desires and listen to Your direction. I'll go where You want me to go today. Help me to focus my energy on Your instruction.

My son, pay attention to what I say;
listen closely to my words. Do not let them
out of your sight, keep them within your heart;
for they are life to those who find them and health
to a man's whole body.
PROVERBS 4:20–22

A DESIRE FOR GOODNESS

God, You are good, and I want to be good. You are like a rock; everything You do is perfect. You are always fair. You are my faithful God who does no wrong, who is right and fair. Let Your goodness drive my life. Help me to recognize sin and call it what it is—*sin*. No more excuses. I refuse to justify wrongdoing just because it's what I want. If it's wrong, it's not from You and I don't want it in my life. Give me a burning desire to hold on tightly to Your righteousness. In all I do, I want to please You.

AN ATTITUDE OF MERCY

Lord, when others treat me unfairly, judge me, or take something I feel I deserved, I want to get even. I want to fight for what is mine, but then I feel You urging me to show mercy. It's hard for me to do that.

> *For the weapons of our warfare are not carnal but*
> *mighty in God for pulling down strongholds, casting*
> *down arguments and every high thing that exalts*
> *itself against the knowledge of God, bringing every*
> *thought into captivity to the obedience of Christ.*
> 2 CORINTHIANS 10:4–5 NKJV

AN ATTITUDE OF REPENTANCE

When I sin, I'm miserable. The weight of my sin puts pressure on my soul. It grips me and makes me feel that I deserve punishment—and I do! But You are always forgiving. Never let me take Your mercy lightly. I'm ashamed, and I don't want to come to You. Give me the courage to tell You the truth about all I've done. Help me to always run *to* You—not away from You—when I fail. Then assure me of Your forgiveness and help me to forgive myself. Thank You for loving me, no matter what!

STRENGTH IN GOD

Praise the LORD! For he has heard my cry for mercy.
The LORD is my strength and shield. I trust him with
all my heart. He helps me, and my heart is filled with
joy. I burst out in songs of thanksgiving.
PSALM 28:6–7 NLT

Lord, I know You hear my voice when I pray to You! You are
my strength and my shield. When my heart trusts in You, I am
overjoyed. You give me courage to meet the challenges of the day.
You give me strength to do the tasks You have set before me. You
build me up, raise me to the heights, and lead me to places I never
would have dreamed were possible. You are the Friend who will
never leave me, the Guide who walks before me. With You in my
life, I can do anything.

NO WORRIES

"I am leaving you with a gift—peace of mind and
heart. And the peace I give is a gift the world cannot
give. So don't be troubled or afraid."
JOHN 14:27 NLT

Lord, it's hard to find peace in this world. Help me not to be
distracted by the noise without and within. Once I come to You,
within the stillness of these early morning hours, my thoughts,
heart, and spirit will be at rest. When I find You and abide within
You, I have no worries, no troubles, no fears. Ah. . . You are peace.
You are life. You are the way.

MY BIBLE—THE POWER OF GOD'S WORD

Adventure, danger, romance. . .just a few story themes from the bestselling book of all time. Undoubtedly, billions of copies have been printed and distributed.

Unlike fairy tales, this book is true and starts with "In the beginning." Here you learn of kings and conquerors, love and loss, rebellion and redemption. Turn the pages to discover where you came from, why you are here, and where you are going. You'll find how to handle money and have better relationships. Most importantly, you can learn who God is and how you can live with Him forever.

What is this astonishing book? The Bible. Inspired by God, this sixty-six-book compilation is the true story of God's love for all people, including you and me. It's the explanation of a promised deliverance, and freedom for all who obey.

"All Scripture," according to 2 Timothy 3:16–17, "is God-breathed and is useful for teaching, rebuking, correcting and training in righteousness, so that the man of God may be thoroughly equipped for every good work." The Bible is the believer's instruction manual for living.

The Bible is sacred and revered—because it is life-giving and powerful. Despite the opposition of modern culture, God's Word stands strong, providing truth in an age of relativism, light in the darkness of deception or depression, and cool refreshment for the challenge of everyday living. Scripture provides encouragement, convicts us of wrongdoing, and teaches us how to live in forgiveness, love, and victory.

The power of God's Word is available to you every day. Do you need to break a bad habit or addiction? Do you need to change your attitude or love those around you or have more patience with family? Perhaps you seek a new perspective, or healing for your physical body or broken heart. Could you use more joy and less stress in your life? The Bible offers healing and comfort, truth and perspective, and the power to transform lives. In other words, the power to live each day and a hope for the future.

Power for supernatural living comes as we ingest God's Word, feeding on it as we would a delicious meal. Let it nourish you as spiritual food. Reflect on it, meditate on it, speak and pray it aloud in your quiet times with the Lord. Commit key verses to memory so you will have them when you need comfort or strength. Finally, take action. *Live* the words you've read. Jesus said, "If you love me, you will obey what I command" (John 14:15).

Like a stone dropped into a pond, the ripple effect of a loving, obedient response to God's Word can go far beyond what you may ever know—in your own life, in your family, in your community, your nation, and your world.

GOD'S WORD IS TRUTH

To the Jews who had believed him, Jesus said, "If you hold to my teaching, you are really my disciples. Then you will know the truth, and the truth will set you free."
JOHN 8:31–32

Thank You, Lord, that Your Word is true. Sometimes it's hard to discern truth from a lie, or even from the half-truths that bombard me daily from the television, radio, magazines, and popular culture. I want to know the truth and live it. Help me to look to Your steady and solid Word, not to this world, for my life instruction manual. I thank You that You will never lead me astray, that You never lie to me, and that You always keep Your promises.

LIGHT FOR UNDERSTANDING

Your word is a lamp to my feet and a light for my path.
PSALM 119:105

Lord, Your Word is a lamp in my darkness—a flashlight on the path of life that helps me see the way. Your words enlighten me with wisdom, insight, and hope, even when I cannot see where I am going or how things will turn out. I'm so glad that You know the right direction. You have gone before me and are always with me, so I don't need to be afraid. I choose to follow Your leading.

DEVOTED TO GOD'S WORD

Today I choose Your Word, Lord. Your way is just and right. I will take the path You have chosen for me, and I will walk in the direction Your Word tells me to go. Help me to follow You with all my heart. Help me to keep my heart right so I always do what pleases You. Help me to keep Your commandments. Show me biblical truths. I am devoted to Your Word. I take it to heart so I will not sin against You.

THE WAY OF TRUTH

Lord, give me understanding so I can know You better. Help me to keep Your commandments and obey Your truth with all my heart. I want to become passionate about Your Word. Turn my heart toward Your desires for my life. In Your truth I find comfort and peace. Turn my eyes away from worthless things and keep my focus on You. Your truth speaks clearly to me every day so I can live my life according to Your will.

GOD'S WORD IS POWERFUL

For the word of God is living and active. Sharper than any double-edged sword, it penetrates even to dividing soul and spirit, joints and marrow; it judges the thoughts and attitudes of the heart.
HEBREWS 4:12

Thank You for Your life-changing words that reveal the true condition of my heart. I can't hide it from You, for You already know everything. But with Your conviction comes repentance and forgiveness. You accept me as I am and give me the grace and power to make real and lasting changes in my life. The Word of God is living and active. That's why it has so much power. I give You my thoughts and attitudes and ask for healing.

EQUIPPED FOR GOOD WORK

All Scripture is God-breathed and is useful for teaching, rebuking, correcting and training in righteousness, so that the man of God may be thoroughly equipped for every good work.
2 TIMOTHY 3:16–17

Lord, I want to have all of the equipment I need to live this life as a Christ-follower. Your Word tells me that You breathed Your life into the words that men put on parchment—which are now the words of the Bible I read. Teach me, Lord. Help me to accept Your rebuke when I need it. Correct and train me in righteousness so that I will be ready for whatever life holds for me today.

LIFE FOR YOUR SOUL

Your Word is perfect, Your principles long-standing and proven over many lifetimes. You revive my soul with Your wise and trustworthy commands. Your Word fills my heart with joy. Lord, help me to realize my mistakes, and please forgive my hidden sins. May the words of my mouth and the meditation of my heart be pleasing in Your sight. You steady me in troubled times with the truth of Your Word (Psalm 19:7–14).

TO UNDERSTAND THE BIBLE

Scripture promises that I can have the mind of Christ so I can know and understand Your words. God, direct my heart and mind as I study and pray. Show me the things I need to comprehend. Make Your wisdom known to me. Help my heart and mind to be fixed on You. Give me great joy in discovering who I am in Christ and the plan You have for my life.

WISDOM IN INTERPRETATION

*Do your best to present yourself to God as one
approved, a workman who does not need to be
ashamed and who correctly handles the word of truth.*
2 TIMOTHY 2:15

Lord, I am Your student. Teach me to read Your word, meditate
on it, and apply it to my life. Give me a hunger for spending time
with You—and wisdom when I teach Your Word to others. I
want to be a person who correctly handles the Word of Truth. I
ask the Holy Spirit to enlighten me and give me understanding
that I may live right and bring glory to Your name.

TO KNOW GOD'S WILL

*For this reason, since the day we heard about you, we have not stopped
praying for you and asking God to fill you with the knowledge of
his will through all spiritual wisdom and understanding.*
COLOSSIANS 1:9

Lord, I want to know Your will for my life. Enlighten me with
wisdom, discernment, and understanding. I need to know when
to stay and when to go, when to speak and when to close my
mouth. Fill me with the knowledge of Your best for me—right
now and in the future. As I seek to follow You, help me to
obediently and joyfully accept Your answers.

WATER THE WORD

As I study the Bible, the seeds of Your Word are planted in my heart. I pray that Your truths deepen in me. Just as a tree grows strong planted by a river filled with good nutrients, I grow stronger each day through the water of Your Word. I will never fail because Your Word lives in me and Your Word will never fail. When I gave my life to You, Lord, You started a good work in me, and I know that it will continue until You return.

GUIDED BY TRUTH

I trust You, Lord, with all my heart. In everything I do, I acknowledge You and give Your Word first place in my life. I walk in the light of Your Word, stepping where You shine the light of truth, trusting I am in the right place at the right time to live my life according to Your purposes. I refuse to veer to the right or the left, but take comfort in knowing that You are always guiding me. I listen as Your voice speaks to me, showing me the way to go.

REVIVE ME!

The law of the LORD is perfect, reviving the soul. The statutes of the LORD are trustworthy, making wise the simple.
PSALM 19:7

Lord, sometimes life gets so crazy. I get so tired and stressed out from working hard at my job—whether it's in the home or in the marketplace. I long to bask in Your presence and find refreshment. Revive my soul with Your Word. Immersed in Your life-giving truth, turn the dark places in my life to light so I can radiate Jesus in my corner of the world.

GIVE ME JOY

The precepts of the LORD are right, giving joy to the heart. The commands of the LORD are radiant, giving light to the eyes.
PSALM 19:8

Lord, Your words are right and true; they bring joy to my heart. I need more joy in my life. Happiness comes and goes, but joy is deep and lasting. This world can take so much out of me with the cares of the day, pressures from my job, and commitments I've made. I need Your true joy despite my circumstances and my feelings. Your commands illuminate me so I can sing Your praises and live revitalized each day. Thank You for Your joy, Lord.

INTEGRITY OF THE WORD

Father, I have great respect for Your Word. I give it first place in my life. Your Word is my umpire, settling disputes and answering questions that I face every day. I refuse to compromise. I set my heart upon the foundation of Your Word and will not be moved from it.

Do not let this Book of the Law depart from your mouth;
meditate on it day and night, so that you may be careful to do
everything written in it. Then you will be prosperous and successful.
JOSHUA 1:8

LIMITLESS POWER OF GOD'S WORD

Thank You, God, for giving me Your Word—Your promise for all eternity. I choose to trust and believe Your Word above all else. I build my faith and hope on You and the power of Your Word. It is alive and working in my life. I know that when I speak Your truths and apply faith, Your Word will accomplish what You sent it to do in my life.

MY BLESSINGS—THE POWER OF ASSURANCE

The Bible is full of God's blessings for our lives, full of positive words, promises granted to those who choose to follow Him, who choose to believe in His assurance. Hebrews 11:8 (NKJV) tells us that "by faith Abraham obeyed when he was called to go out to the place which he would receive as an inheritance" and that "he went out, not knowing where he was going." And when Abraham arrived at his destination, God *met him there* and gave him a brand-new promise: "I will bless you. . .and you will be a blessing" (Genesis 12:2 AMP). As sons and daughters of Abraham (see Galatians 3:7), we share in this promise! We can be filled with assurance that wherever we go, God will bless us. He is even going before us, ready to greet us with a word of encouragement when we get there.

Is your faith strong enough and your mind open enough to make room for God's bounty of blessings? Or is your faith too little, your mind too closed? Perhaps you feel you are undeserving. If so, plant the words of Hebrews 11:6 (AMP) in your heart: "Without faith it is impossible to please and be satisfactory to Him. For whoever would come near to God must [necessarily] believe that God exists and that He is the rewarder of those who earnestly and diligently seek Him [out]." Claim the promise of 1 John 5:14–15 (NKJV): "Now this is the confidence that we have in Him, that if we ask anything according to His will, He hears us. And if we know that He hears us, whatever we ask, we know that we have the petitions that we have asked of Him." It's not a matter of deserving but of firm faith, great expectation, and sincere seeking.

Thank God for eternal promises, past blessings, and the assurance of blessings to come. By doing so, you'll avoid the pitfall of seeing the world through eyes of discouragement. Andrew Murray wrote, "The faith that always thanks Him—not for experiences, but for the promises on which it can rely—goes on from strength to strength, still increasing in the blessed assurance that God Himself will perfect His work in us." Praise and thank God for all His blessings, focusing on the Giver and not on the gift.

During your quiet time, make a list of how the Lord has blessed you in the past. Then make a list of the blessings you anticipate in the present and the future. Don't buy into a negative mind-set. Believe that God has good things out there just waiting for you to open your arms to receive them. Empty yourself of disbelief and discouragement. Revel in the power of assurance that God is ready and willing to bless your life. And be sure to pray for an opportunity to be a blessing to others.

Choose to believe that Christ loves you and is blessing you even in the midst of trials. He always goes before you, planting blessings on your path. God "daily loads us with benefits" (Psalm 68:19 NKJV). Your job: Claim them today.

SHARING MY BLESSINGS

"Every man shall give as he is able, according to the
blessing of the LORD your God which He has given you."
DEUTERONOMY 16:17 NASB

Lord, You have blessed me and the works of my hands. I am so grateful to You for all that I have. As You bless me, I am able to bless others in whatever way I can. What a feeling to know that I am able to help expand Your kingdom! Help me to tithe my talents, monies, and time, all to Your glory. For thine is the kingdom and the power, forever and ever.

OBEDIENCE AND BLESSINGS

Obey the LORD your God so that all these
blessings will come and stay with you.
DEUTERONOMY 28:2 NCV

I hear Your voice, Lord, and I thank You for the blessings that You have showered upon me. Sometimes I feel so unworthy, but You love me so much that at times I cannot understand it. All that You have blessed me with goes beyond me, as I respond to Your voice, do Your will, and work to serve others. Speak to me, Lord. Tell me whom, what, and where You want me to bless. I am Your servant, Lord; speak to me.

AN AWESOME GOD

It is Your presence, Your blessings, Your love that makes my life so rich and fulfilling. I am not worried about what others have and I have not. I am full of joy for what I do have—mainly You! There is nothing greater than You, Lord. You are an awesome God. Nothing I do can make You any greater than Your word and Your promises. I praise You for what You are doing in my life, for making me rich beyond my wildest dreams as I live and breathe in You.

DAILY BENEFITS

I am loaded with benefits! Blessed beyond compare! You, the God of my salvation, the Friend who laid down His life for me, the One who is with me in fire, flood, and famine, the One who will never leave me or forsake me! Today is a new day, and You have benefits waiting out there for me. I begin the day in my walk toward You, leaving my burdens behind and focusing on the benefits ahead. And when I come to You at the close of the day, You will be waiting for me, at the end of the path, with a good word.

GUARANTEED BLESSING

"The LORD will guarantee a blessing on everything you do."
DEUTERONOMY 28:8 NLT

Your Word says that You actually *guarantee* a blessing on everything I do! That's a promise I can count on, and one I revel in. It gives me the confidence that You will be with me in all that I do, blessing me at each and every turn. What an awesome promise! I arise today, assured of Your assistance, guidance, and approval of every good thing. There are no words to express how You make me feel. I am humbled in Your presence and renewed in Your light. I praise You, Lord!

CHOOSING LIFE

"I call heaven and earth as witnesses today against you,
that I have set before you life and death, blessing and cursing;
therefore choose life, that both you and your descendants may live."
DEUTERONOMY 30:19 NKJV

Lord, this day I choose life—I choose to live and work and have my being in You. Instead of looking at all that I don't have, I choose to look at all that You have blessed me with—family, friends, a home, a job, clothes on my back, food in my belly.... Oh, Lord, the list is endless. Thank You so much for being my life, today and every day! I cling to You each and every moment. Live through me!

THE LAW OF SOWING AND REAPING

"Bring to the storehouse a full tenth of what you earn so there will be food in my house. Test me in this," says the LORD All-Powerful. "I will open the windows of heaven for you and pour out all the blessings you need."
MALACHI 3:10 NCV

Lord, Your Word says it is true—the more I give, the more I get. Yet that's not why I do it. I give of myself to bless others because that is what You have called me to do. The more I step out in Your Word, with You walking before me, the more I am blessed by Your presence and Your promises. It's not all about material things, although those are blessings as well. But I am more focused on the spiritual, for that is what keeps me close to You, unshaken, undisturbed, unfettered. Praise to Your holy name!

HEAVENLY BLESSINGS

All praise to God, the Father of our Lord Jesus Christ, who has blessed us with every spiritual blessing in the heavenly realms because we are united with Christ.
EPHESIANS 1:3 NLT

Because I am united with Your Son, who gave His life so that we could live, You have blessed me with every spiritual blessing. Here I sit at my Savior's knee, His hand upon my head. I am at peace. I am blessed. I am in the heavenly realms. Here, nothing can harm me, for He has blessed me beyond measure. Lord, my cup runneth over with love for You!

MY JOB

Do not do wrong to repay a wrong, and do not insult to repay an insult. But repay with a blessing, because you yourselves were called to do this so that you might receive a blessing.
1 PETER 3:9 NCV

My job—to bless others. What an awesome privilege to be an extension of Your arm. To bless others, who don't even know I am the blesser! That's so cool. To do these things in secret, not wanting to be known, fills me with so much pleasure. There is nothing like it. Show me whose lives I can bless today, even in the simplest of things.

BLESSING ENEMIES

Wish good for those who harm you; wish them well and do not curse them.
ROMANS 12:14 NCV

God, I pray that you will bless those who have not been kind to me. You know who they are. Give me the blessing of forgiving others as You always forgive me. Help me not to repay evil with evil, but to repay evil with good, for that is what You would have me do. Give me the strength to be kind to them, even helpful, and to keep my anger and frustration at bay. Bless their lives, Lord. In Jesus' name I pray.

JOYFUL IN HOPE

Lord, I thank You for giving me hope. I don't know where I would be without You. I don't know what the future holds, but You give me the ability to be joyful even while I wait—even when I don't understand. Please help me to have a positive attitude and live with a mind-set of patience and courage as You work Your will in my life. Help me to remain faithful in prayer, Lord, and fully committed to You.

JOY

Our mouths were filled with laughter,
our tongues with songs of joy.
PSALM 126:2

Lord, thank You for the gift of laughter! I thank You for the joy You bring into my life through a child's smile, a luscious peach, a hot bath, and a good night's sleep. Help me remember that when I am "looking up" to You, Lord, I can have a more optimistic outlook and be a more positive person. Keep my eyes on You, not myself or my circumstances, so I can live with a lighter, more joy-filled heart.

PRAISE YE THE LORD

May the peoples praise you, O God; may all the peoples praise you.
Then the land will yield its harvest, and God, our God, will bless us.
PSALM 67:5–6

I praise God from whom all blessings flow. You bless us beyond measure; we the sheep of Your pasture. You give us green meadows in which to lie down, calm waters to give us rest. You forgive us our sins. You love us beyond measure. There is no greater blessing than Your presence in my life, than Your desire to hear of all my troubles, cares, and woes. You are here to lift the burden from my shoulders and shower blessings down upon me. I praise the name of Jesus in whom I cannot but trust.

A DAILY BENEDICTION

"The LORD bless you, and keep you; the LORD make
His face shine on you, and be gracious to you; the LORD
lift up His countenance on you, and give you peace."
NUMBERS 6:24–26 NASB

May You walk down the road with me today. May You shower my path with Your many blessings. May You keep me from danger. May Your light keep me from the darkness surrounding me. May You give me grace and peace and strength for the day. May You give me someone to bless as You have blessed me. May You be there, waiting for me, at the end of the day with a good word to calm my spirit as I rest in Your arms.

THE RIGHT FOCUS

Lord, I am thirsty, parched with the demands of this world. I am in want in so many ways. Help me not to focus on what I don't have, but to focus on You and the blessings that You have prepared for me and my children. Pour out Your Spirit upon me now. Fill me with Your presence. Give me hope for this day. I anticipate blessings waiting around every corner. Thank You, Lord, for taking such good care of me. You, my Savior, are the greatest blessing of all!

A SYMBOL AND SOURCE OF BLESSING

Lord, Your Son has already rescued me! I am so full of joy! You have made me both a symbol of that blessing and a source of blessing to others. I am not afraid of things in this world for I am assured of Your promises. I will be strong, confident in the benefits You bestow upon me, able to stretch myself as I strive to reach others so that they, too, will have the benefit of Your blessings. What power! What confidence! What hope!

MY BODY—THE POWER OF PURITY

A little boy, not more than three years old, looked up at his grandpa. "Papa, do you have Jesus in your heart?" he asked. "Yes," his grandpa replied. The little boy looked at the cigarette in his grandfather's hand and said, "So, are you making Jesus smoke?"

The apostle Paul, in 1 Corinthians 3:16, asks a similar question: "Don't you know that you yourselves are God's temple and that God's Spirit lives in you?" In a world where sex sells every product imaginable, it can be tough to stand for purity and modesty.

Have you ever watched a horror movie and found it stayed with you? You probably knew you shouldn't watch it, but you convinced yourself it wouldn't bother you. Yet once those images were imprinted on your mind, they were difficult to forget.

You—spirit, soul, and body—are what you eat. Your spirit and mind respond to what you put into them just as your body responds to what you put into it. Caffeine might give you energy, or turkey might make you tired. What you see and hear affects you, too. What you think about fills your mind and enters your heart.

That's why the Bible is clear that we are to think about "whatever is true, whatever is noble, whatever is right, whatever is pure, whatever is lovely, whatever is admirable," things that are "excellent or praiseworthy" (Philippians 4:8).

When you expose yourself to things that contradict what you say you believe, it damages your heart. Your old nature—who you were before you knew the Lord—craves those things that are counter to God. And when you feed the old nature, it gains strength; and at the same time, you starve your spirit from the things of God.

God has set some guidelines in His Word that will keep you on the right road for your life. However, you're going to make mistakes. We all do. The key is to run *to* God instead of *away* from Him when you fail. He loves you more than you can ever know—but you have to trust that He will forgive you and give you a second chance. . .and a third. . .and a fourth. His mercy is new every morning.

As you choose to remain faithful to God, that commitment brings freedom from the negative things that can attach themselves to your life. "And so, dear brothers and sisters, I plead with you to give your bodies to God because of all he has done for you. Let them be a living and holy sacrifice—the kind he will find acceptable" (Romans 12:1 NLT).

A RIGHT PERSPECTIVE

Father, sometimes I wish I looked different, because there are things about my body that I don't like. Remind me that You knew what I looked like long before I was born. I am wonderfully made by Your hand. Help me to be thankful for how You designed me. I want to be a good steward of the body You gave me. Help me to nurture it, respect it, and celebrate it. My body doesn't belong to me—it belongs to You! And what I do with it reflects on You.

What agreement is there between the temple of God
and idols? For we are the temple of the living God.
As God has said: "I will live with them and walk among
them, and I will be their God, and they will be my people."
2 CORINTHIANS 6:16

SET APART

Father, I belong to You. My life—spirit, soul, and body—belongs to You. Forgive me when I choose my own way. When I give in to my own selfish desires, I not only hurt myself; I hurt You. Remind me that I'm set apart for You.

FOR MY BODY

God, You created my body and gave it to me as a gift. Teach me how to keep it healthy. Give me wisdom and strength to make right choices. Teach me what Your Word says about my body and help me to do what is right. Show me how to control my passions and my appetites so I can live a long and healthy life. Protect me from dangerous addictions. I don't want to be dependent on anything or anyone but You. Help me to be fit for Your service, ready at a moment's notice to do what You ask.

TO BE SEXUALLY PURE

Lord, forgive me for the sins of my past. Cleanse me and make me pure. Help me to honor You in all my relationships so that, when the time comes to give myself to my spouse, I can do so with integrity of heart. Help me to keep myself for my spouse until the day You unite our hearts as one.

FREEDOM FROM PORNOGRAPHY

God, I am responsible for what I put in front of my eyes. It is my responsibility to protect myself. Forgive me for looking at pornography. I am ashamed and feel guilty, but am compelled by it. I need help. Give me courage to go to someone I trust who will pray for me and help me be accountable. Show me who that person is. Heal my heart and make me clean again. Convict me when I'm tempted, and draw me close to You. I look to You—You are where my help comes from.

FREEDOM FROM SEXUAL SIN

Father, forgive me. I feel like I'm damaged and beyond repair. I've destroyed something precious and I can't take it back. I'm disappointed in myself for believing the lie that sexual sin was okay. Forgive me for justifying it. I was wrong. Heal my heart and give me hope again.

FOR A PURE HEART

God, create in me a pure heart and a right spirit. Show me all my wrongdoings. Give me the strength to resist the lies that distort my thinking when I try to justify sin. Make me new, like the first day I was born into the kingdom of God. As I fill my mind with Your truth from the Bible, help me to renew my mind with right thinking. Show me Your ways and instruct me in all I do. Guide me with Your eye and direct me with Your truth.

The temptations in your life are no different from what others experience. And God is faithful. He will not allow the temptation to be more than you can stand. When you are tempted, he will show you a way out so that you can endure.
1 CORINTHIANS 10:13 NLT

WHEN I'M TEMPTED

Father, You have promised me a way of escape. I am listening and I want a way out. Help me to stand against all that tempts me. Help me always to choose You over temptation.

FREEDOM FROM SUBSTANCE ABUSE

God, forgive me for trying to find comfort in drugs or alcohol to escape reality. I justified it because of the pain I was feeling, and I was wrong. I should have come to You instead of looking to other things to solve my problems. Help me to discern the flaws in my heart that need to change so I can overcome this temptation. Open my heart and expose the truth to me so I can change. Remind me that I can run to You with my problems. You have the answers I need for my life.

FINDING A SECURE PATH

Lord, fill me with Your strength and direct my ways so I can successfully press through the temptation of sin. I want to remain obedient to Your leadership. I don't want to take Your mercy and grace for granted. Help me to focus on what is pure and holy in Your sight.

PRAYERS OFFERED IN FAITH

*Is anyone among you sick? Then he must call for the elders of the church
and they are to pray over him, anointing him with oil in the name of
the Lord; and the prayer offered in faith will restore the one who is sick.*
JAMES 5:14–15 NASB

Lord, I am feeling so poorly. You know what is attacking my
body. You can see everything. I ask you in prayer, right now, to fill
me with Your healing light. Banish the sickness from my body.
Fill me with Your presence. Draw me unto You.

THE HEALING EDGE

*People. . .begged him to let the sick just touch the
edge of his cloak, and all who touched him were healed.*
MATTHEW 14:35–36

Lord, when I connect with You, when my body is filled with Your
power and love, nothing can harm me. I am healed from within.
Fill me now with Your presence. Heal my body, soul, and spirit.
I praise Your name, for You are the one who heals me, saves me,
loves me! Thank You for giving me life!

STRENGTH IN WEAKNESS

Therefore I take pleasure in infirmities, in reproaches,
in needs, in persecutions, in distresses, for Christ's sake.
For when I am weak, then I am strong.
2 CORINTHIANS 12:10 NKJV

It's a paradox, but it is Your truth. When I am weak, I am strong because Your strength is made perfect in my weakness. Because You are in my life, I can rest in You. With Your loving arms around me, I am buoyed in spirit, soul, and body. When I am with You there is peace and comfort.

I WANT TO BE LIKE JESUS

And we know that in all things God works for the good of those who
love him, who have been called according to his purpose. For those God
foreknew he also predestined to be conformed to the likeness of his Son.
ROMANS 8:28–29

Lord, I know that You will work everything out according to Your glory, according to Your will. I feel privileged that You have chosen me to serve You, that You have called me to this life. I want to be like You. Give me the strength of Christ, for His grace is sufficient for me. Thank You for hearing my prayer. Oh my soul, rejoice!

TO YIELD TO GOD'S STANDARDS

Lord, You know me better than I know myself. You know my internal struggles and the things that challenge me deep within my soul. You created me, and You know what I need. I surrender what I want for what You know I need. You have the highest standards, and I want to meet them. I give myself to Your will and hope with great expectation to live my life according to the standards You have set in place.

I urge you, as aliens and strangers in the world,
to abstain from sinful desires, which war against your soul.
1 PETER 2:11

PURITY IN MY SPEECH

Father, You created me to be pure like You. Please forgive me when I allow the impure language of the world to come out of my mouth. I have polluted my heart by allowing those thoughts to penetrate my mind. Remove that trash from my heart as I fill up on scriptures. I am responsible for the words I speak. Help me to ask others who heard me speak like that to forgive me as well. A trash-talker is not who I want to be. When I say words like that, I am not a reflection of You.

MY CHALLENGES—
THE POWER OF FAITH-BASED BOLDNESS

The youngest of Jesse's sons, David, spent many hours in the fields, taking care of his father's sheep. It was here that David prayed and meditated on God, his constant Companion. His reliance on God to deliver him from lions and bears in the wild was evidence of the intimate relationship David had developed with God at an early age. This intimacy with the Lord allowed David's faith to grow. David knew God would be with him in every situation. It was his faith that gave him the boldness to do whatever God called him to do.

When David left his father's fields to check on his brothers who were with King Saul's army, it was not by chance that his visit coincided with the appearance of the nine-foot-nine-inch-tall Philistine warrior named Goliath, who was defying the army of Israel. As David began talking to the soldiers, he encountered his first challenge in the form of his oldest brother, Eliab, who said, "Why have you come down? And with whom have you left those few sheep in the wilderness? I know your insolence and the wickedness of your heart; for you have come down in order to see the battle" (1 Samuel 17:28 NASB).

David's next confrontation was with King Saul, who "from his shoulders upward. . .was taller than any of the [other children of Israel]" (1 Samuel 9:2 NKJV). Now, you'd think that because of his size, Saul himself would have fought Goliath. Instead, Saul tried to discourage the only one willing to face the giant. Saul said to David, "There's no way you can fight this Philistine and possibly win! You're only a boy, and he's been a man of war since his youth" (1 Samuel 17:33 NLT).

John Maxwell wrote, "A successful person is one who takes the cold water dumped on his plans, heats it with his enthusiasm, and manufactures the steam to push ahead." Our David was so successful in refuting Saul's discouraging remarks that the king himself became enthusiastic and said to him, "Go, and the LORD be with you" (1 Samuel 17:37).

Unlike Saul and Eliab—the kind of people who see such a large problem in front of them that they are unable to comprehend the possibility of either licking it or avoiding that particular obstacle—David was able "to boldly go where no man has gone before." Because of his intimate knowledge of God, David was able to turn away from a maligner, defend himself before a discourager, and fell a giant intimidator with one smooth stone. By using faith-based boldness, David met the challenges presented to him and, as a result, routed the entire Philistine army. All for God's glory!

Tim Elmore wrote, "It has been said that new challenges cause you either to freeze or to focus." But if we build up our confidence by spending time in the Word, prayer, and meditation, getting to know our God intimately, we can be like David, who with faith-based boldness "rose early in the morning" (1 Samuel 17:20 NKJV) to meet every challenge God put in his path.

DISSUADED FROM YOUR GOAL

*They were just trying to intimidate us, imagining
that they could discourage us and stop the work.
So I continued the work with even greater determination.*
NEHEMIAH 6:9 NLT

Lord, here I am trying to take on this work and others are
trying to intimidate me, telling me there is no way I can meet
the challenge You have set before me. But I have faith in You. I
know that with You in my life, I can do whatever You call me to
do. Help me not to let others dissuade me from my goal. Give
me the faith that David sought from You, the kind that does not
waver but goes boldly forward.

BOLD AND DILIGENT

I'm working as hard as I can to meet my challenge. I want to
do my best, knowing that You are with me all the way. Help
me to be brave. Help me not to panic. Neither fear nor anxiety
is of You. I need to focus on You, to build up my faith and my
confidence. Help me not to deviate from my course. I am here
this morning, ready to listen to Your voice. Lead me, gentle
Shepherd, where You want me to go.

FACING THE UNKNOWN

Oh Lord, I feel called to take on this new challenge. I can feel the Spirit drawing me into this latest endeavor. But I don't know what's going to happen. Oh, how I sometimes wish I could see into the future. Lord, help me to have confidence, trust, and faith in Your will for my life. Help me to just put one foot in front of the other, to do the next thing, to continue walking in Your way. And when I get there, I will give You all the glory!

FEARLESSNESS

Though an army may encamp against me,
my heart shall not fear.
PSALM 27:3 NKJV

I remember the story of David, how he faced opposition from his brother, his king, and then a huge giant, all under the watchful eyes of his enemies. But he was not afraid. Oh, that I would have such faith. Sometimes I get so scared my heart begins beating a mile a minute. And those are the times when I have taken my eyes off of You. Keep my focus on Your Word. Plant this verse in my heart so that when dread comes upon me, I can say these words and kiss fear good-bye.

STANDING WITH GOD

Everyone deserted me. May it not be held against them. But the Lord stood at my side and gave me strength. . . . And I was delivered.
2 TIMOTHY 4:16–17

All of a sudden, I am as alone as David when he stood before Goliath. But I am not going to be mad at others for deserting me. I don't need them. All I need is You. You are my Lord, my Savior, my Deliverer, my Rock, my Refuge. You are by my side. I can feel Your presence right here, right now. Oh, how wonderful You are! Thank You for giving me the power I need. Thank You for never leaving me.

SUPPORT OF FELLOW BELIEVERS

*When [Paul] would not be dissuaded,
we gave up and said, "The Lord's will be done."*
ACTS 21:14

Sometimes those who don't know You think that believers like me are crazy. But we're not. We just know that when You call us to do something, when You put a challenge before us, we are to go forward with no fear. We are bold in You, Lord! How awesome is that! And thankfully, fellow believers encourage us, knowing that if it is Your will, all will be well. What would I do without that support? Thank You for planting my feet in a broad place, surrounded by fellow believers who love and pray for me.

OUR HELP

Our help is in the name of the LORD,
who made heaven and earth.
PSALM 124:8 NKJV

I need look no further than You, Lord, to help me. It is Your
name that I trust. It is Your power that will help me meet this
challenge. After all, You made heaven and earth. You made me.
You know the plan for my life. You have equipped me to do what
You have called me to do. Help me not to rely on myself but on
You and Your power. That is what is going to give me victory in
this life. Thank You for hearing and answering my prayer.

MY ARMOR

I will not trust in my bow, nor shall my sword save me. But You have
saved us from our enemies, and have put to shame those who hated us.
In God we boast all day long, and praise Your name forever.
PSALM 44:6–8 NKJV

I do not trust in my talents, diligence, money, education, luck, or
others to help me meet this challenge. I trust in You. My power
is in the faith-based boldness that comes only from knowing You
intimately. With that weapon in my arsenal, there is only victory
ahead. Those who say I cannot do what You have called me to do
will be put to shame. But that's not why I continue to meet this
challenge. I go forward because I want to bring glory to you. It is
in You that I boast all day long. I praise Your name, my Strength
and my Deliverer.

HOPE

"And now, Lord, what do I wait for? My hope is in You."
PSALM 39:7 NKJV

Some hope in employers or money or connections or that one big break. I hope in You and what You want to do through me while I'm here on earth. Don't let me drag my feet in fear but let me boldly run forward as David did when he faced Goliath. David knew You, and he knew that You would always be with him, no matter what. That's a fabulous faith. That's faith-based boldness! Empower me with that today so that I, like David, can go out with You and take on giants.

MAKE ME BOLD

On the day I called, You answered me;
You made me bold with strength in my soul.
PSALM 138:3 NASB

Sometimes I feel like a ninety-five-pound weakling when it comes to my faith. I let my doubts and fears overtake me and then find myself shrinking from the challenges You put before me. Lord, I ask You to make me bold. Give me the strength to take on all comers. To do what You want me to do. Dispel the darkness that surrounds me. Warm me with the light of Your face. Bring me to where You want me to be. Give me strength in my soul!

BY FAITH, I GO

By faith Abraham, when he was called, obeyed by going
out to a place which he was to receive for an inheritance;
and he went out, not knowing where he was going.
HEBREWS 11:8 NASB

In these days of online direction services and personal navigation
systems, I can't imagine not knowing where I am going. What
Abraham might have given for a map! But that's what faith is all
about, isn't it? It's the substance of things hoped for, the evidence
of things unseen (see Hebrews 11:1). So give me that faith, Lord,
as I take on this challenge. I don't know where it will lead or how
it will all turn out, but by faith I will obey this call You have put
upon my life. I will go out, not knowing, because I trust in You!

AT THE THRONE

So let us come boldly to the throne of our gracious God.
There we will receive his mercy, and we will find
grace to help us when we need it most.
HEBREWS 4:16 NLT

Here I am again, Lord, coming boldly before You, kneeling at
the foot of Your throne. I need Your mercy this morning, and
although it seems like I ask for this over and over again, give me
more faith, Lord. Help me not to run from this challenge. Give
me the grace, strength, energy, talent, and intelligence that I need
to make this come out right. I come to You, bowing down, asking
for Your love and power to fill me and give me the strength I
need to accomplish the challenges before me this day.

GOD LOOKS AT THE HEART

But the LORD said to Samuel, "Do not consider his appearance or his height, for I have rejected him. The LORD does not look at the things man looks at. Man looks at the outward appearance, but the LORD looks at the heart."
1 SAMUEL 16:7

Some people look at me and say, "There's no way you can do this." But with You I can do anything, Lord. You don't just look at my appearance. When You look at me, You look directly at my heart. I know that You have made me to use my particular talents to accomplish particular tasks here on earth. You know my purpose, my path. Help me use all my resources to meet this challenge before me. All to Your glory!

IN GOD'S STRENGTH

It's amazing—I can do all things through You! You give me the power! You give me the energy! You give me the ways and the means! As I lie here, in Your presence, I feel all the energy emanating from You. Oh, what a feeling! Give me that strength I need to accomplish the goals You set before me. Plant the words "I can do all things through God—He strengthens me!" in my heart forever and ever.

KEEP MY TONGUE FROM EVIL

I want to enjoy life! I want to see good days! But to do that, I need to keep my tongue from evil and my lips—my eternally flapping lips—from negative words, lies, and malice. There is no way I can do this by myself. No, I need Your Spirit to fill me with love and peace and joy. I need Your hand to guide me. I need Your mind to dwell within me. Give me the strength, grace, and peace I need to speak to others today in Your wisdom and Your truth.

THE GOOD WORDS

Then our mouth was filled with laughter,
and our tongue with singing. Then they said among
the nations, "The LORD has done great things for them."
PSALM 126:2 NKJV

You have filled my mouth with laughter! My tongue is singing Your praises! Others see me and say, "Wow! Look at what the Lord has done for her!" This is amazing. I am so alive in You this morning. And it is because I am not only praying and reading Your Word, but also allowing You to live in me and putting Your Word into action. It can't get any better than this, and it's all because of Your sacrifice, Your dying for me. Thank You, Jesus, for making me whole and happy in You.

MY CHURCH—THE POWER OF CHRISTIAN FELLOWSHIP

Ask many people to picture the word *church*, and they'll envision a building with a steeple. To them, a church is a place to conduct a worship service. Yet the church isn't simply a building, nor is a worship service limited to activities inside a structure. The word *church* isn't found in the Old Testament. Jesus uses the word for the first time in the New Testament. He speaks of the Church with a very specific meaning. The Church is the body of believers. He uses several examples to describe His relationship to the Church. He says He is the vine and His followers are the branches (see John 15). He also refers to the Church as His body. These images show how closely believers are joined with Him and with one another. Romans 12:5 says, "So in Christ we who are many form one body, and each member belongs to all the others." Jesus is the head of the Church. The Church refers to all of those people worldwide who have accepted Jesus as their Savior. Often, however, the word also means a group of local individuals who meet regularly to worship God. In either case, the Church is a body of Christians who are in fellowship with Jesus and with one another. The first record of a church service is found in Acts 2:42: "They devoted themselves to the apostles' teaching and to the fellowship, to the breaking of bread and to prayer."

God created the church to have an impact on both the believers and their communities. In this assembly we are encouraged to improve our service to the Lord. Singing, praying, studying the Bible, and engaging in other Christian activities are ways to worship God. At the same time, these activities strengthen our faith and refresh us in our determination to lead holy lives. Sometimes we think of the worship service as requiring our attendance, and we walk away from it believing we've done our duty for the week. But worship extends beyond the weekly assembly. Offering a friendly smile, exercising patience in trying times, and giving an even-tempered reply to harsh words are as much acts of worship as are singing songs and listening to the Gospel. The assembly of believers takes on additional importance when we think of it as a training ground that prepares us to enter the world and bring Jesus to those who are without Him.

The institutions built by humans—governments, schools, businesses, organizations, and societies—attempt to solve the world's problems. But without the application of Christian principles, they have limited success. To the community, the church exemplifies the blessings that come from being in fellowship with Jesus. To bring light to our neighbors, we need our spirits to be habitually renewed. Regular meetings with other Christians afford the opportunity to experience such renewal. The Bible reinforces the importance of meeting with other believers in Hebrews 10:25: "Let us not give up meeting together, as some are in the habit of doing, but let us encourage one another—and all the more as you see the Day approaching."

CHURCH FAMILY

Lord, I pray for my church family. Give us strength to put aside our differences so we can serve You together. Help us to understand and care about one another—just as You care about each one of us. Show me who I can learn from and who should be learning from me. Place me where You want me to be within Your family.

FINDING A CHURCH

God, I need a church home. I want to share my faith and learn Your wisdom by spending time with other believers. Guide me to a church where Your truth and love are practiced, not just preached. Help me to be bold and to be first to reach out to people You want me to get to know. Thank You for providing me with friendships that will grow my faith and give me an opportunity to receive support for the challenges I face. Give me discernment so I know where I belong within Your family.

BODY OF CHRIST

"Although I am less than the least of all God's people, this grace was given me: to preach to the Gentiles the unsearchable riches of Christ, and to make plain to everyone the administration of this mystery, which for ages past was kept hidden in God, who created all things. His intent was that now, through the church, the manifold wisdom of God should be made known to the rulers and authorities in the heavenly realms, according to his eternal purpose which he accomplished in Christ Jesus our Lord" (Ephesians 3:8–11).

LOVE FOR THE CHURCH

Lord, I appreciate Your love for the church. You make Yourself known to us through the fellowship of believers. We are the works of Your hands, and our best attributes are a mirror of Your qualities. When we come together, help us reinforce those characteristics that best reveal Your nature. You are our ultimate model, but seeing others reflect Your love strengthens us as well. I pray I will reflect the light of Your love.

TO GO BEYOND THE FOUR WALLS

Jesus, I need Your help. We have become comfortable inside our church. Where is the desire to tell others about You? Teach us how to go outside the four walls of our church building. Speak to the hearts of the people within our church family. Share Your vision to reach out into the community through them. Give us the desire to demonstrate Your love to those who are hurting. Grow in us an eagerness to reach and transform lives through the love of God within us.

> *"For where two or three come together*
> *in my name, there am I with them."*
> MATTHEW 18:20

MORE PRAYER

Father, You said Your house would be a house of prayer. I ask You to put a burning desire in the hearts of Your people to pray and seek You. Help us to be diligent to pray for You to heal our land, as You promised to do if we prayed. It's great to see people at church, but our purpose is not a social function. We get together to focus on You. Teach us to pray for the things that concern You.

RESPECT FOR OTHERS

Lord, help me radiate a warm acceptance of fellow Christians. May they delight in meeting with me. Never should they feel that I'm examining their words or actions for hidden motives. Let my attitude show respect for their opinions and their service to You. May others leave my presence feeling that they have become more solid in their walk with You. I would be pleased if they become better people because they have known me.

IMAGE OF CHRIST

Lord, help me cultivate a strong bond with other church members. Guide me in developing confidence in them. Help me be reliable so that they, too, have confidence in me. It's vital that we act with one spirit and one purpose. Should we become cold toward one another, assist me in being the first to recognize the peril and to work to restore fellowship before unity is lost. Keep me focused not on myself but on You so that Christian love prevails.

HONOR FOR LEADERS

Dear Father, a person is honored to be a Christian and doubly honored to be a Christian leader. Blessed is the church that has loyal leaders who honestly seek after the truth. With the encouragement of their followers, they can concentrate on keeping their eyes fixed on You; we become a congregation with one spirit and one purpose. They need my support. They are due my respect. Give me the humility to accept and embrace their leadership.

CHRISTIAN FELLOWSHIP

Father, I enjoy the fellowship of Christians. They believe in me and influence me to do better. In a world of suspicion and ulterior motives, it's a welcome relief to be in the company of those who choose to see me in the best light. They accept the sincerity of my purpose without bias. I'm refreshed in their presence. I pray I will honor Your church by enhancing their strengths rather than dwelling on their weaknesses.

SENSELESS CRITICISM

Lord, the church must do Your work, yet every action is an opportunity for criticism. I find flaws far too easily. I can argue with others about simple matters. Even successful efforts can be criticized because they are not outstanding enough. Turn me away from expressing disapproval that serves no purpose. Teach me to appreciate what others do. Develop in me the resolve to replace words that lead to disharmony with dialogue that supports unity.

THE CHURCH'S PRAYER FOR BOLDNESS

"When they heard this, they raised their voices together in prayer to God. 'Sovereign Lord,' they said, 'you made the heaven and the earth and the sea, and everything in them. You spoke by the Holy Spirit through the mouth of your servant, our father David: "Why do the nations rage and the peoples plot in vain? The kings of the earth take their stand and the rulers gather together against the Lord and against his Anointed One"'" (Acts 4:24–26).

FREEDOM TO WORSHIP

Heavenly Father, elsewhere in the world today, Christians face danger merely because they believe in You. To assemble as a church requires courage. I'm so blessed to gather with other Christians in freedom. Meeting with others to worship rekindles my spirit. Father, I desire to take the freedom of worshipping You beyond the church meeting place. Help me extend my faith and infuse my everyday life with service to You.

CHOOSING THE BEST COURSE

Lord, effective Christian action grows in an atmosphere of encouragement. In our work, many questions arise, such as which programs to support and how best to direct our efforts. I pray Your grace will be with all those in my church. Steer us along the best course between the rocks of hard-line fanaticism and the murky waters of caution. May we work as an agreeable team to bring honor to Your name.

FOR MY PASTOR

God, thank You for giving me a spiritual leader who loves me and You. Help him to always speak Your truth and never stray from it. Surround him with wise counsel, and give him a heart that listens to counsel that ultimately comes from You. Keep him close to You, filled with Your compassion for the people You have placed in our church. Protect him from criticism. Help him to be watchful over our church family, discerning what is Your best. Bless him and his family in everything they do.

TO BE A SUPPORT TO OTHERS

Lord, help me to encourage others every day. Help me to share what I have with others and encourage them. You are my strength, so I will lean on You as others lean on me. Help me to build their faith instead of tearing it down. Help me to be positive and uplifting when people share their troubles with me. When people leave my presence, I want them to feel better than when they came to see me.

MY DREAMS AND GOALS—
THE POWER OF SURRENDER

Do you remember daydreaming as a child about what you wanted to be when you grew up? Most of us do. Whether we thought we'd be ballerinas or baby doctors, movie stars or marine biologists, many of us have lost track of our dreams. Perhaps fear kept us from taking risks, or lack of motivation, money, or time held us back. What we wanted to become—and not necessarily just our occupational choices—got derailed.

Whatever the reasons, it's never too late to dream again and discover God's will for the next season of our lives.

Maybe you've always wanted to start your own business or go back to school.

Perhaps your desire is to find pursuits that are more rewarding, like volunteering or mentoring youth. Maybe you'd really like to have more time together as a family. Or, if you're single, perhaps you'd like to find a man with whom you are well matched, someone to share life with. Maybe it's time for a change, but you just don't know how to get from where you are now to where you'd like to be.

"More things are wrought by prayer than this world dreams of," said Alfred Lord Tennyson. Praying powerfully for our goals requires us to first surrender them to God, being willing to accept God's plan no matter what the outcome. Jesus Christ surrendered with His words and His actions when He prayed with his face on the ground, "My Father, if it is possible, may this cup be taken from me. Yet not as I will, but as you will" (Matthew 26:39). God didn't answer the prayer of His own Son in the way Jesus wanted.

Instead, He led Jesus to something incomprehensibly hard, yet ultimately glorious. God's no became a bigger yes for the entire human race. We may not always understand God's ways, but we can take comfort in knowing that when God delays—or redirects—it is for a good reason.

As we seek God's will for our dreams and goals, we ask Him to confirm if we are headed in the right direction. Psalm 37:23 says, "If the LORD delights in a man's way, he makes his steps firm." That verse puts an image of a frozen Minnesota lake in my mind: If you take a step and the ice is solid, you keep walking. But if the ice begins to crack and break under your feet, you know it's wise to go another direction. God plants dreams in our hearts, and as we stay connected to Him in prayer, He reveals direction for every step of the way.

Prayer is the key to reaching our goals no matter what phase of the journey we're in—planning, working, or "living the dream." Prayer gives us patience, guidance, and direction. When we commit our dreams to God (Psalm 37:4–5), we can pray powerfully with sincere and surrendered hearts. We plan our work and work our plan—and trust God with the entire process.

DARING TO DREAM

*Delight yourself in the LORD and he
will give you the desires of your heart.*
PSALM 37:4

Dear Giver of Dreams, I believe you've placed dreams within me that are yet to be realized. Teach me to delight myself in You as I pursue the desires of my heart. Show me Your perfect will—may I move as far and as fast as you wish, never less or more. Grant me the wisdom I need to accomplish Your plans for my life, and the humility to give You the glory in them.

KNOWING GOD'S WILL

*Do not conform any longer to the pattern of this world, but be
transformed by the renewing of your mind. Then you will be able to test
and approve what God's will is—his good, pleasing and perfect will.*
ROMANS 12:2

Lord, I commit my aspirations to You. Give me the courage to work toward my own goals, and not to be swayed by the opinions of others. Renew my mind and my spirit so I will be able to test and approve what Your will is—Your good, pleasing, and perfect will. I don't have to be afraid that I will miss it—I can know that You bring people and circumstances into my life for a reason. Thank You for the assurance that You will direct me into Your good purposes.

THE GOD WHO CARES

You discern my going out and my lying down;
you are familiar with all my ways.
PSALM 139:3

Lord, I thank You that You are the God who cares! You want the best for me and You are constantly designing the next steps of this journey of my life. Powerful, yet gentle and kind, You delight in giving us dreams—and the resources to achieve our goals. I pray for dreams that are worthy and wonderful. Empower me, gracious God, to be a woman of action who trusts You.

THE GIVER OF GUIDANCE

I will instruct you and teach you in the way you should go;
I will counsel you and watch over you.
PSALM 32:8

Lord, I appreciate Your wise hand of guidance. You instruct me and teach me in the way I should go; You counsel me and watch over me. What a blessing! What a privilege! No one knows my inner heart and life dreams like You, Lord. Still me. Help me to listen so I can hear Your direction. And when I hear, give me the courage to walk forward knowing You are always near. You are with me every step of the way, Lord.

TRUSTING GOD'S WISDOM

For the LORD gives wisdom, and from his
mouth come knowledge and understanding.
PROVERBS 2:6

Lord, what a blessing it is to be able to come before You—the wisest, most intelligent Being in the universe. I have direct access, straight to the top. Thank You for giving me wisdom and direction, even when I can't see the way. Knowledge and understanding come directly from Your mouth, Lord, and You delight to enlighten us. I praise You and ask for continued insight as my dreams become achievable goals.

MAKE LOVE YOUR AIM

The goal of this command is love, which comes from
a pure heart and a good conscience and a sincere faith.
1 TIMOTHY 1:5

Lord, in all my activity to achieve my goals, through the effort and the trusting, may my highest aim be love. Love is Your greatest commandment. Fill me with Your unconditional and accepting love and empower me to care deeply and well for others. May the love I give come from a pure heart, uncontaminated by selfishness. Help me to have the right motives and be genuinely and sincerely concerned about other people's lives.

NOTHING IS TOO HARD FOR GOD

"I am the LORD, the God of all mankind.
Is anything too hard for me?"
JEREMIAH 32:27

Lord, I want things to be different in my life—but there are so many obstacles. I need energy and motivation to get going. I need finances and more time. More than anything, I need to trust You more. Nothing is too difficult for You, Father. You can do anything! Despite all my needs and distractions, please bring into my life favor and openings—please make a way. I ask that You would help me achieve the goals in my life that are best suited for Your good purposes.

BEING A PERSON OF ACTION

In the same way, faith by itself,
if it is not accompanied by action, is dead.
JAMES 2:17

Lord, I want to be a person of action—a person of true faith. Faith by itself—if only thoughts and words—is dead. It has to be accompanied by my deeds, Lord. I pray for the wisdom to know when to take risks, when to act, and when to wait. Help me to know the right thing to do and the best time to do it. Put true faith into me, Lord, so I can perform the good works You have for me to accomplish.

TRUSTING GOD'S PLANS FOR MY LIFE

"For I know the plans I have for you," declares the LORD, "plans to prosper you and not to harm you, plans to give you hope and a future."
JEREMIAH 29:11

Lord, You are the faithful God. I have hope for my future because of Your good promises. On You I rely. Reveal to me Your good plans for my life. As I share my dreams and visions with You, please mold them into reality—or mash them like clay on a potter's wheel into something more than I ever could have asked for or imagined. I put my trust in You, Lord.

GOD IS FAITHFUL

The one who calls you is faithful and he will do it.
1 THESSALONIANS 5:24

Lord, I thank You that You are my faithful God. No one else is like You. People move away, jobs change, and much of life is uncertain. But You are always here, my stable, loving, and present Lord. Help me to hold unswervingly to the hope I profess, for You alone are faithful. You keep all Your promises—every one of them, all of the time—and I thank You for that, Lord.

SURRENDERING YOUR DREAMS

*Going a little farther, he fell with his face to the ground
and prayed, "My Father, if it is possible, may this cup
be taken from me. Yet not as I will, but as you will."*
MATTHEW 26:39

Lord, I humbly bow before You and give You my dreams. I give
up control. I surrender my will for Yours. When I am tempted
to do things my way, may I seek Your guidance instead. When I
am too pushy, trying to make things happen on my own, give me
mercy to see that Your grace has everything covered. I don't have
to be afraid, Lord. I will trust You to meet my every need.

PATIENCE FOR "IN THE MEANTIME"

*Be patient, then, brothers, until the Lord's coming. See how
the farmer waits for the land to yield its valuable crop and
how patient he is for the autumn and spring rains.*
JAMES 5:7

Lord, it's hard to wait. There are so many things I want, and
I'm inclined to charge ahead and "get it done." But You give
us the "meantime" season for a reason. I ask for the patience
and courage to wait well. Help me to be a woman of wisdom,
knowing You have reasons for Your delays. You are not just
killing time, Lord—You are ordering events and shaping my
character. I yield to Your timing, Father.

MY EDUCATION—THE POWER OF KNOWLEDGE

Just because you've graduated doesn't mean it's time to stop learning. You may be surprised to find that being a willing student outside the classroom is just as important as the time you spent cracking the books in school.

Everything God created was made to grow, and that includes your wisdom and understanding of the things of God. As a Christian, you will forever be a student of His. You even have your own personal instructor, the Holy Spirit. "You have received the Holy Spirit, and he lives within you, so you don't need anyone to teach you what is true. For the Spirit teaches you everything you need to know, and what he teaches is true—it is not a lie. So just as he has taught you, remain in fellowship with Christ" (1 John 2:27 NLT).

The Spirit of God is diligently at work doing a makeover within your heart so you become a reflection of His image, but He needs your cooperation. Reading the Bible fills your mind with what God says and thinks. When you make Bible time a priority, it will cause you to grow in your faith quickly. Through His Word, you are constantly discovering who He is and who He created you to be.

Your prayer life is your lifeline to growing in God. As you spend time talking to Him and listening to His voice speak to your heart, you come to know Him.

Jesus said, "I tell you the truth, the man who does not enter the sheep pen by the gate, but climbs in by some other way, is a thief and a robber. The man who enters by the gate is the shepherd of his sheep. The watchman opens the gate for him, and the sheep listen to his voice. He calls his own sheep by name and leads them out. When he has brought out all his own, he goes on ahead of them, and his sheep follow him because they know his voice. But they will never follow a stranger; in fact, they will run away from him because they do not recognize a stranger's voice" (John 10:1–5).

Just as you know the voices of those who love you—your family, close friends, and others—you come to recognize the voice of God. In the same respect, when a stranger speaks, their voice is unfamiliar to you, just as the stranger's voice was unfamiliar to the sheep. You grow in your relationship with God and learn to respond to His direction as He teaches you the way He wants you to go and what He wants you to do.

The more time you spend with Him, the more aware you are of His presence. As you find out more about Him, you uncover the characteristics within yourself that reflect His likeness. His direction and guidance will help you be successful as you transition to your next step in life.

TO KNOW YOU, LORD

Heavenly Father, I am Your child. I belong to You. I want to know You more. Give me understanding of who You are and what You are like. Teach me the things that are important to You so they can become important to me. Help me to put You first in my life. Give me wisdom to choose time with You and to eliminate distractions that keep me too busy for You.

> *"I want you to show love, not offer sacrifices. I want you to know me more than I want burnt offerings."*
> HOSEA 6:6 NLT

TO HEAR HIS VOICE

God, I want to hear Your voice. I want to know You are speaking to my heart about Your will for my life. Just as the sheep follow the shepherd's voice and pay no attention to the stranger's words, help me to shut out strange voices so I may hear You clearly. Give me patience to listen—and not talk. What You have to tell me is much more important than what I have to say. Help me to practice Your presence and wait on You. Nothing is more important than time with You.

TO UNDERSTAND THE BIBLE

The Bible is Your Word for my life. Help me to understand what You are saying to me through it. Give me wisdom and understanding as I allow scripture to feed my spirit and fill me with Your strength. I read Your words so I can grow and learn more about You. Bring the words I read back to mind when I need to apply them to the circumstances I face.

You made me and formed me with your hands.
Give me understanding so I can learn your commands.
PSALM 119:73 NCV

LIVING IN THE REAL WORLD NOW

School used textbooks to prepare me for the world, but now it's time to experience it for myself. Give me wisdom and help me to apply what I've learned in school to my new environment outside the classroom. Prepare me for the things school didn't prepare me for. Be with me in every situation and show me how to deal with each day, making good decisions and right applications for a successful life.

LEARNING TO TALK TO YOUR BOSS

Lord, thank You for my job and for giving me the support of my boss. Sometimes it can be intimidating to talk to my supervisor. I hate it when my mouth goes dry and my hands get sweaty. Fill me with Your confidence. Give me words to speak and the courage to say the things that need to be said. I was hired to do a job, and I will do it well because I know You are with me.

Trust in the LORD with all your heart;
do not depend on your own understanding.
PROVERBS 3:5 NLT

ASKING FOR HELP

Lord, You know I hate asking for help, but I need to learn to rely on others. Some things I can't do by myself, and You created me to need other people. Direct me to the ones I should ask for help. Remind me to appreciate their help and not take it for granted. Give me words to express how much their assistance means to me. Help me to be open-minded if the way they want to help is not what I expected.

TO KNOW THE TRUTH

Lord, thank You for making absolute truth available. You came into the world to testify for truth. It is not relative to what I think or feel. Truth is objective and is based on Your Word, the Bible. Help me to know the truth and see it clearly in my life.

We know also that the Son of God has come and has given us understanding, so that we may know him who is true. And we are in him who is true—even in his Son Jesus Christ. He is the true God and eternal life.

1 JOHN 5:20

FOR MENTORS

God, You put people in my life to mentor me. Give me discernment so I know who is a gift from You and who is not. Help me to open up to mentors and receive their counsel. Forgive my pride when I think I know the answers. Let me learn from their mistakes as well as their successes. Help me to be a good student. Teach me to apply Your principles to my life and recognize them as I experience the road You have destined me to travel.

SEEKING THE RIGHT KNOWLEDGE

God, You know everything. All I want to know is already known by You. Teach me to seek truth in a way that pleases You. I don't want to use what I *think* I know of You or Your Word to look good in front of other people. Help me to keep my motives pure. I never want to seek knowledge that is separate from You. Help me to know You by listening to You and observing what You do. I don't just want to know Your Word; I want to put it into practice. I want to live it out loud every day.

DISCOVERING LEADERSHIP

Heavenly Father, I want to understand how to become a leader. Jesus led by serving others. He gave of Himself freely to show us the way to truth. Teach me what it takes to lead as I begin by following You and the leaders You have placed in my life. Give me a heart to serve and the patience to not take shortcuts in the lessons You want me to learn.

PAYING ATTENTION

God, as I am learning and growing in You daily, teach me to be attentive to Your instruction. Do not let me forget what I have learned from You. Remind me of the amazing and miraculous things You have done to bring me to where I am today. Help me to stand firm in my faith, not just knowing what I believe, but living it. Keep me alert and cautious about people or things that would distract and hinder me from growing in You.

A CONCENTRATED FOCUS

Lord, fatigue is the enemy of my faith. I refuse to grow weary in my walk with You. Help me to make You the center of all my activities. Give me a clear perception of my relationship with You, that I may learn Your ways and understand my place in Your plan. Like a beam of light breaks through the darkness, break through my mental fog, Lord, and teach me how to focus my attention on You.

LEARNING IN THE CIRCUMSTANCES

God, teach me how to tune out the voice of my circumstances, the busyness of my life, and the noise surrounding me. My situation hasn't changed, but my attitude has. My hope is in You. Help me to focus on Your promises instead of the circumstances that are shouting at me. I open my heart to listen to Your instruction. Teach me to go to the still waters of Your Spirit and find strength. Peace like a river speaks to me.

THE POWER OF WISDOM

Father, I am listening to Your instruction. I will hide Your Word in my heart, and I will not forget what You have done for me. I want to experience Your blessings. I will keep Your commandments, not just because You said to, but because I love You. Give me Your wisdom, Lord. Help me to gain understanding.

DEVELOPING A PASSION FOR THE BIBLE

Father, help me to make daily Bible study as much a part of my life as eating. Remind me that the Bible is more than a book, that it contains words revealing Your love for me. Holy Spirit, speak to my heart and tell me what I need to discover each day. Bring what I've read back to my memory so I can meditate on what Your Word is saying to me personally.

BEING PASSIONATE ABOUT THE RIGHT THINGS

Forgive me, Lord, when I am tempted to love things that are pretty to look at or make me feel good about myself. I want to stay focused on You. Help me to eliminate anything that competes with knowing You. Remind me when my natural desires are not in line with what You would have me pursue. I want to love what You love and hate what You hate. Help me to get rid of things in my life that keep me from serving You with all that I am.

MY EMOTIONS—THE POWER OF A RENEWED MIND

Brandon has a successful career in financial services. After his sixty-hour workweeks, he rarely has the energy to initiate friendships. Instead, Brandon arrives home late, pops a frozen dinner into the microwave, flips on the television, and sinks into the couch until bedtime. While he is pleasant and competent at the office, Brandon is lonely and isolated in the rest of his life.

Erin is angry, though she doesn't want anyone to know that. Her two teenage daughters—once her sweet, carefree little girls—are disobedient and disrespectful. They like to party every night, even during the school week, and Erin feels helpless to stop them. She wants her friends to think she's a competent mother, so she hides her emotions with a continual smile. Like a duck gliding across the water, she appears calm on the surface—but in reality, she's paddling wildly just to stay afloat. Erin wants to scream, "Doesn't anyone know how much pain I'm in?" But instead she replies with a cheery, "Oh, I'm fine!" when anyone asks how she's doing.

Emotions are a normal part of life. As human beings, each of us has a full range of emotions—love, happiness, joy, delight, peace, disappointment, loss, grief, doubt, compassion, sadness, depression, jealousy, anger, bitterness, guilt, and many others. We are happy when a friend comes to visit, we are sad when our dog dies, and we are frustrated when we can't seem to lose weight.

Throughout the Bible, women and men—even Jesus—displayed a variety of emotions. I imagine that Adam and Eve were deliriously happy in the Garden of Eden. The woman caught in adultery and pushed before a condemning crowd must

POWER Prayers *for Your Life*

have felt humiliation. Mary, the virgin mother of Jesus, was fearful when she learned she was pregnant, then joyful when she discovered the news was true—she would give birth to the Savior of the world! David was afraid for his life while Saul pursued him with murderous intent. And Jesus felt alone, broken to the point of sweating blood, as He prayed for His life to be spared.

Emotions, whether positive or negative, can be powerful—even overwhelming at times. Managing those emotions is a part of maturity. When our emotions aren't processed in healthy ways, they can get stuck like a clogged drain. Help comes when we surrender our feelings to the One who has the power to blast away our emotional congestion.

Prayer is essential to managing emotions. Praying powerfully for this area of our lives can begin with praying 2 Corinthians 10:5, asking God to help us "take captive every thought to make it obedient to Christ." To change how we feel, we need to change how we think. When we change the way we view our situations, we can change the way we respond to them—with wisdom, rather than impulsive actions we may regret later.

With God's help, we can get through both the valleys and the victories of life.

GOD AND EMOTIONS

"The LORD is slow to anger, abounding in
love and forgiving sin and rebellion."
NUMBERS 14:18

Lord, what a blessing You are that You have given us such an array of emotions with which to express ourselves. Help me to be more like You—slow to anger and abounding in love. Help me to be a woman who is forgiving. I pray for more discernment, so that in whatever comes my way I will have the grace to think, speak, and act with a good and godly attitude.

RENEWING YOUR MIND

Do not conform any longer to the pattern of this world, but be
transformed by the renewing of your mind. Then you will be able to test
and approve what God's will is—his good, pleasing and perfect will.
ROMANS 12:2

Lord, sometimes I feel like my emotions need a makeover. Renovate me—transform me so I can be balanced and healthy in my emotions. I ask for your power to change. I don't want to be the way I used to be. I want be wise and enjoy sound thinking. I want to make good decisions in how I express myself in my words and actions. Help me to know Your will and have a mind that's renewed.

LOVE FOR OTHERS

Dear friends, let us love one another, for love comes from God.
Everyone who loves has been born of God and knows God.
1 JOHN 4:7

Lord, You are the author of love. As I read Your Book and
discover what love really is, help me receive it and express that
love for others. Teach me Your ways. You are so good at loving
people—You are kind, compassionate, interested, accepting,
and nonjudgmental. You seek the best for other people. You
empathize with their joy and sadness. You make them feel
special. Lord, let me be a person who loves like that, too.

CONFIDENCE

Have no fear of sudden disaster or of the ruin
that overtakes the wicked, for the LORD will be your
confidence and will keep your foot from being snared.
PROVERBS 3:25–26

Lord, I want to be more confident. I don't want to be afraid
of disasters—or just making mistakes. Give me the courage to
know that You, Lord, will be my confidence. You keep me from
tripping over my tongue and saying the wrong thing. But even
when I do, You have the power to make things right again. Thank
You for the confidence You give me. Let me walk with my head
high because I know who I am in Christ: I am Yours!

COMPASSION

Be kind and compassionate to one another,
forgiving each other, just as in Christ God forgave you.
EPHESIANS 4:32

Lord, Your compassion for people is great. You healed the blind and You led the people who were lost like sheep without a shepherd. Create in me a heart of compassion—enlarge my vision so I see and help the poor, the sick, the people who don't know You, and the people whose concerns You lay upon my heart. Help me never to be so busy or self-absorbed that I overlook my family and friends who may need my assistance.

NEEDING ENCOURAGEMENT

May our Lord Jesus Christ himself and God our Father, who loved
us and by his grace gave us eternal encouragement and good hope,
encourage your hearts and strengthen you in every good deed and word.
2 THESSALONIANS 2:16–17

Lord, I need encouragement. Will You please inspire my heart and strengthen me in everything I say and do? I need Your truth to lift my spirit and help me soar. Let me be like an eagle that glides on the wind. Give me the courage and energy I need to keep going, even when I'm weary.

STRESS

*Cast your cares on the L*ORD *and he will sustain you;*
he will never let the righteous fall.
PSALM 55:22

Lord, I can't take one more day of this hectic whirl of life—the traffic, the crying kids, my workload at the office, and everything else I have to handle. Sometimes, it just feels like too much! Help me to breathe out my cares, casting them away like line from a fishing rod. But don't let me reel them back in! Here is my burned-out, anxious heart. May Your oceans of love and power replenish me, providing the energy I need to do what You want me to do each day.

LONELINESS

"Surely I am with you always, to the very end of the age."
MATTHEW 28:20

Lord, I thank You that You are my true companion—that I am never alone. You have assigned angels to watch over and protect me. You have given me your Holy Spirit and promised that You are with me always, even to the very end of the age. What a privilege that You call me Your friend. As we travel this road of life together, on city sidewalks, suburban roads, or country paths, I enjoy your presence, Lord. Help me never to forget Your presence.

ANGER

Get rid of all bitterness, rage and anger,
brawling and slander, along with every form of malice.
EPHESIANS 4:31

Lord, I am so mad! I am angry and I need Your help. Why do things have to go so wrong? I need to do something with this heated emotion—and I choose to give You my anger and bitterness, Lord. Help me be rid of it. Redeem the confusion and bring peace to what seems so out of control. Free me from resentment and blame. Show me my part in this conflict as you speak to the heart of my nemesis. I need your healing and peace, Lord.

HEALING GUILT AND SHAME

Day and night your hand was heavy upon me. . . . Then I acknowledged
my sin to you and did not cover up my iniquity. I said, "I will confess
my transgressions to the LORD"—and you forgave the guilt of my sin.
PSALM 32:4–6

Lord, my shame makes me want to hide. But I can no longer hide in the darkness of my guilt and sin. You already know everything I've done wrong, yet you bring me into the light— not to condemn, nor to condone, but to heal me. I acknowledge my wrongs and confess them all to You, Lord. I stand in Your forgiveness as the cleansing water of Your gentle love flows over me, washing away my guilt and shame.

SADNESS

Why are you downcast, O my soul? Why so disturbed within me?
Put your hope in God, for I will yet praise him.
PSALM 42:5

Lord, I feel so gloomy today. Do you see my tears? In my sadness, help me to remember that even when I'm down, I can choose to put my hope in You. Instead of telling myself lies that push me deeper into despair, I can look to Your truth. Remind me of the good things you have done in the past. I choose to praise you. You are my Savior and my God. May Your love comfort me now.

DEPRESSION

He lifted me out of the slimy pit, out of the mud and mire;
he set my feet on a rock and gave me a firm place to stand.
He put a new song in my mouth, a hymn of praise to our God.
Many will see and fear and put their trust in the LORD.
PSALM 40:2–3

Lord, will you please change the music of my life from a sad, minor key to a joy-filled, major key? Give me a new song to sing, a happier tune! It's amazing to me that there is no mess too big for You to fix, no broken life too shattered for You to restore, and no loss too great for You to redeem. As You raise me out of the darkness of my slimy pit, lifting me from the mud and mire of my depression to solid emotional ground, I will praise You.

MY FAITH—THE POWER OF KNOWING GOD

How many times have you taken a seat in class, plopped down on a couch, or leaned back in a recliner without a second thought as to whether the furniture would hold you? You had no expectation of it letting you hit the ground unless you'd had an experience of falling. Then you might second-guess your faith in that chair, couch, or recliner.

Faith in what we can see is easy for us. We live in a natural world, and we rely on our five senses to tell us what to expect from the things we do each day. We expect the engine in our car to start when we turn the key. We expect our tires to hold air, and we trust that other drivers will obey the traffic lights and road signs.

The natural can fail us, and does. Yet while we see accidents on the road every day because others fail to obey the law, we still expect to come and go each day safely.

Our faith in the unseen should be even stronger. Spiritually we should have an even higher expectation to see fulfilled the promises God has made to us; and yet we don't always believe we will receive results when we pray.

Jesus said, "I tell you, you can pray for anything, and if you believe that you've received it, it will be yours" (Mark 11:24 NLT). That promise is from Jesus Christ Himself. Yet day after day we find ourselves doubting because we can't see the fulfillment of our requests.

How many times have you given up on what you've asked God for because you didn't see it in the time frame you expected? God doesn't work on our timetables. Sometimes it takes time, effort, and energy to move circumstances out of the way in order to make a clear path for the things we ask for, much like moving a physical mountain into the sea.

Imagine you were in a park and you threw a Frisbee. You waited for it to come back, but then you became discouraged, disappointed, or distracted, left the park, and went home. Imagine the next day the Frisbee came back, but you were gone.

When you give up waiting for the answer to your prayer request, it's as though you stopped watching for God to throw a Frisbee back. The answer to your prayer is coming back to you, but you're gone. You never waited to receive it.

God does what He does in His own time. You have to be patient and keep believing that He's working behind the scenes to bring answers for your life. He wants to give you the desires of your heart when you pray according to His purposes and plan. Don't quit believing. Keep expecting to receive what you asked for.

PRAISE FOR GOD'S INDESCRIBABLE GIFT

Thank You for giving the most precious gift, Your very own Son, so I could live each day with You. There are no words to describe the depths of Your sacrifice, but I know You did it for me. You gave Your first and only Son so You could share life with many sons and daughters. I am so thankful Jesus was willing to give His life for mine.

"For God so loved the world that he gave his one and only Son, that whoever believes in him shall not perish but have eternal life."
JOHN 3:16

YOUR GIFT ACCEPTED

Jesus, please be the Lord and Savior of my life. I confess my sins to You. Take my life and purge me from all that is ungodly and of this world. Fill me with new life. Make me a new creature, filled with Your Spirit. I willingly give You my life—take it and make it whatever pleases You. Without You I am nothing, but in You I can reach my full potential. Help me to live my life so that I am a reflection of You, pointing others to eternal life with You.

THE FULLNESS OF THE HOLY SPIRIT

Thank You, Lord, for Your Holy Spirit. I trust that the Holy Spirit leads and guides me in every area of my life. You sent the Holy Spirit to comfort me and teach me all things. He directs my steps and helps me to make wise life choices. He shows me God's best for my life. I set my heart on the promise of His presence and diligently listen to His leading.

KNOWING GOD IS THERE

God, I know You are there. Even though I can't see You with my eyes, I sense Your presence when I pray. When I feel alone, I remember Your promise to never leave me. Faith allows me to see the unseen, to trust what I cannot touch. I rely on my spiritual senses to get me through to the other side of the challenges in my life—the challenges that tempt me to doubt You and let go of the truth of Your love. Thank You for always making Yourself known to me when I need You.

TAKE UP YOUR CROSS

Jesus, it takes sacrifice to follow You. I have so many dreams for my life, but they are nothing unless they include You. Help me to let go of the things I selfishly desire and that aren't meant to be a part of my life. Your purposes for my life mean success. I give You my life—I completely surrender.

> *Then he said to the crowd, "If any of you wants to*
> *be my follower, you must turn from your selfish ways,*
> *take up your cross daily, and follow me."*
> LUKE 9:23 NLT

FINDING FAITH

Father, the Bible says every person has been given a measure of faith. I already have faith—You instilled it in me when I gave my life to You. Sometimes I don't feel as if I have much faith, especially when I wonder how You could possibly turn my messy life around. But You are always faithful, and I have to remember all You have already brought me through. Help me to grow in faith. Help me to remember that the more I trust You while facing difficulty, the stronger my faith becomes.

ASKING FOR GOD'S HELP

Sometimes I feel You have so much on Your plate that I should work things out on my own. I know I shouldn't feel like I'm bothering You, but my problems seem small compared to what others deal with. Still, I know You want to help me. You are just waiting for me to ask, so I'm asking—please help. You know what I'm dealing with. Forgive me for not coming to You sooner. I accept Your help today.

God is my helper; the Lord is
with those who uphold my life.
PSALM 54:4 NKJV

KNOWING GOD'S MERCY

Father, You love me with no strings attached. No matter what I do or don't do, You show me grace that makes me love You more. Everywhere I turn, Your eyes are on me, caring for me with a compassion greater than the love I could ever experience from anyone else. Thank You for Your promise that Your mercy follows me all the days of my life.

SEEING THE UNSEEN

Lord, I am learning so much. I want to see You in the small moments in my life today. I don't want to take anything for granted, so show me the majestic beauty of Your creation. I want to experience You in all I see. Help me to see the unseen. Give me wisdom to read and understand Your Word. Give me discernment so I know the right things I should do. Open the eyes of my spirit so I can see clearly from Your perspective.

THE POWER OF GOD'S PROTECTION

Fairy tales and fables always have a hero—a rescuer, protector, and conqueror. God, You created me and gave me life. You are the One who saves my life every day. You have given Your angels charge over me to keep me protected. You go before me and fight my battles, sometimes without me ever knowing those battles exist. You are my refuge and my shield. Thank You for always being there.

INCREASE MY FAITH

Jesus, You promised if I believe when I pray according to our Father's will, then I can have what I ask. It's so hard to believe sometimes, especially when it seems my prayer is taking a long time to be answered. Forgive me for not trusting You. You have never failed me, and sometimes I forget that. Help me to stand in faith, knowing that I will see the results of my faith. Remind me that answers come in Your time, not mine. You are the finisher of my faith, so I hold tight to You.

THE POWER OF GOD'S CLOSENESS

God, I am depending on my own abilities. I don't want to feel far from You, but I do. Yet being close to You is more than a feeling. As I draw closer to You, I know You will draw closer to me. Your presence gives me an inner strength that is not my own. Let me experience You as if You were standing close enough that I could feel Your breath on my face.

STRENGTHENED IN THE FAITH

Just as you received Christ Jesus as Lord, continue to live in him, rooted and built up in him, strengthened in the faith as you were taught, and overflowing with thankfulness.
COLOSSIANS 2:6–7

Jesus, my Jesus, thank You for always being with me, holding me up above the waters of this life, especially when the current is more than I can bear. As You uphold me, day by day, morning by morning, my faith grows. There is no one like You, Jesus. No one like You. I am strengthened during this time with You. I overflow with thankfulness and praise. What would I ever do without You in my life?

OPEN EYES, ENDLESS HOPE

I pray that the eyes of your heart may be enlightened, so that you will know what is the hope of His calling, what are the riches of the glory of His inheritance in the saints, and what is the surpassing greatness of His power toward us who believe.
EPHESIANS 1:18–19 NASB

Each morning You open the eyes of my heart and fill me with Your awesome resurrection power. As I seek Your face, I am filled with endless hope. I revel in Your glorious riches. I am saved by the power of belief. Enlighten my mind, heart, and spirit as we spend these moments together. I await Your words, dear Lord. Speak to me now!

EXPERIENCING GOD'S STRENGTH

Life's demands seem heavier than ever before. I am taking a moment right now to recharge my soul with Your strength. Remind me that my help comes from You—whatever I need. You are my power source, and I plug in right now. Fill me up physically, mentally, and emotionally. Thank You that I don't have to go through my life alone. You are always there to recharge me when my power supply is running low. I rest in You today.

God is my strength and power,
and He makes my way perfect.
2 SAMUEL 22:33 NKJV

PRAYING GOD'S WORDS

I don't have to worry about my problems today. You are giving me the answers I need to change my life. Hebrews 4:12 says, "The word of God is living and active. Sharper than any double-edged sword." When I speak and pray the scriptures, I am agreeing with You in what You want to do on the earth and in my life. I attach my faith to Your words, and You give life to the desires of my heart. As I pray today, I know Your power is released to answer my prayers.

MY FAMILY—THE POWER OF WORDS

Words have power. We can use words to heal or harm, lift or lower, teach or taunt. Frederick Buechner wrote, "In Hebrew, the word *dabar* means both word and deed. A word doesn't merely say something, it does something. It brings something into being. It makes something happen."

When you talk to your family, are your words building them up or tearing them down? Have you said things that you wished you could take back? As Frederick Buechner wrote, "Words spoken in deep love or deep hate set things in motion within the human heart that can never be reversed."

What steps can you take to ensure that you are feeding your family, your children, a healthy conversational diet? First, when communicating, *be quick to listen*. Larry Burkett wrote, "How many times have you jumped into a conversation impulsively, to add your two cents, only to regret it later? Remember, 'He who gives an answer before he hears, it is folly and shame to him' (Proverbs 18:13 NASB)."

Second, *be slow to speak*. Think and pray before you let any words come out of your mouth. Proverbs 16:1 (AMP) says, "The plans of the mind and orderly thinking belong to man, but from the Lord comes the [wise] answer of the tongue." Praying *before* speaking will save you a lot of heartache later.

Ask God to help you gain control of your tongue. Use your words to build up your family members (see 1 Thessalonians 5:11). Honor others—those above (parents, grandparents), beside (spouses), and below you (children and grandchildren)—more than you honor yourself (see Philippians 2:3), by listening to them, praying before you speak, and responding in gentleness.

And if, after an intense discussion, you realize that in spite of yourself you've said some things you shouldn't have, be humble enough to apologize. When you do, chances are good that he or she will be more ready to apologize to you—and to others throughout life. If you "train up a child in the way he should go, even when he is old he will not depart from it" (Proverbs 22:6 NASB).

By the power of your godly words, you can equip your child with three faiths: "Faith in himself. . .that he can do anything which he wants to do if it is done with God's blessing and approval. . . . Faith in you and in all other children of God. . .by setting him the example you want him to follow. . . . Faith in God. . .that God loves him, that God cares for him, that God wants him to be happy."*

In conversation, do not "withhold good from those to whom it is due, when it is in the power of your hand to do so" (Proverbs 3:27 NKJV). When you sit down to talk with your children, listen and then pray for the right words to say in calmness of tone and manner, demonstrating that Christ is at the center of your speech and life.

*Life Study Fellowship, *With God All Things Are Possible* (New York: Bantam Books, 1972), 58, 60–61

MORNING PRAYER FOR GODLY WORDS

The Sovereign LORD has given me his words of wisdom,
so that I know how to comfort the weary. Morning by morning
he wakens me and opens my understanding to his will.
ISAIAH 50:4 NLT

Lord, here I am this morning, awaiting Your words of wisdom. I need to have a talk with my child today, and I don't know what to say or how to say it. Give me direction. Open my eyes, heart, and spirit to understanding Your will for me and my child. I want to know how to speak words to comfort, direct, and assist. Help me, Oh Lord. Guide the words of my tongue.

MADE A MISTAKE

Indeed, we all make many mistakes. For if we
could control our tongues, we would be perfect and
could also control ourselves in every other way.
JAMES 3:2 NLT

Oh God, if only I could control my tongue! My life is more like "open mouth, insert foot." And that's just what I've done. Is there any way to remedy this situation? Help me in this endeavor. Give me the courage to be humble, to go to my child and admit I've made a mistake. May he/she forgive me as I have forgiven my child so often in the past, and as You constantly forgive all of us. Help us put this incident behind us. Give me the wisdom to do better next time. All to Your glory!

WHEN I'VE HURT MY FAMILY

I've made decisions in my life that hurt my family. I didn't mean to hurt them. Please forgive me, and I pray they find it in their hearts to forgive me, too. I know they may never understand—please let that be okay. Heal our hurts for the words we've said to one another. Help us to better understand one another. Help them understand that I have to go my own way—even if that means making my own mistakes. Restore our relationship and open doors so that we can grow together again as a family.

UNSAVED LOVED ONES

It's been difficult serving You when my family members don't know You. I can't seem to make them understand. I don't want to argue or defend my relationship with You anymore. Help me to choose words and actions that let them see You in me. I pray they see the difference You have made in my life and that they'll come to know You, too.

CURB MY TONGUE

The tongue can bring death or life;
those who love to talk will reap the consequences.
PROVERBS 18:21 NLT

Lord, my tongue just went on and on—and now I am reaping the consequences. When will I ever learn when to stop talking? It seems I continually belabor a point until my child has zoned out and becomes unresponsive. Help me to weigh my words carefully, to say only what You want me to say. In other words, help me to zip up my mouth!

JESUS' WORD POWER

[Jesus said,] "The Spirit alone gives eternal life.
Human effort accomplishes nothing. And the very
words I have spoken to you are spirit and life."
JOHN 6:63 NLT

I try and try, but my efforts accomplish nothing when I have not come first to You in prayer. I need to do things in Your strength, for otherwise I am useless. I need Your power behind me when I speak. I need Your strength. Allow Your Word to speak to me. Guide my way by Your gentle voice. May my spirit and Yours become one this day.

FOR PEACE IN MY FAMILY

You have promised the peace that passes understanding. Thank You that Your Spirit lives in and with us. My family is blessed in all we do. I thank You, Lord, that Your peace goes with us. No matter how much chaos is going on around us, we can rest and rely on You. Help us not to get caught up in the moments when it seems the world is spinning out of control. Remind us to fix our minds and hearts on You and live in Your strength today.

FACING A FAMILY CRISIS

It is so hard dealing with this family crisis. Lord, teach me how to face these issues in a positive way. I feel so alone. Thank You for being with me. I can't be the one to fix this problem for them even though I'd like to. You're the only One who can. Bring people across my path who I can talk to about this, people who can support me and lift me up. Help me to focus on what I have to do, and keep me from becoming distracted. I give it all to You right now. I know You won't let any of us down.

KIND VERSUS CUTTING WORDS

Words have cut me to the quick. Now I know how others feel when I harm them with my words. It really hurts. I feel very wounded. My stomach is filled with anger, sorrow, embarrassment, bitterness, and rage. Lord, give me a kind thought from Your Word today, scripture that will heal and build me back up. Take this sorrow from me and replace it with a spirit of forgiveness. Lift me up to Your rock of refuge.

BUILDING UP

Lord, today not one negative thought is going to go through my head and come out my mouth. This morning I will drench myself in Your Word and come out smiling. I want to spread to others the joy You plant in my heart. Give me the right words to say at the right moment to build up others. Give me words of praise, words of wisdom, and words of encouragement.

LIVING MY FAITH

If you claim to be religious but don't control your tongue,
you are fooling yourself, and your religion is worthless.
JAMES 1:26 NLT

Lord, I want to live my faith before my children and others. To do that I need to be able to control my words, but sometimes, although I know this is impossible, my tongue seems to have a "mind" of its own. Help me rein in my mouth. Give me words that will lead my children to You. Help me to live a life that is rich in Your love—and may that love affect my speech. Begin with me this morning and show me how to live this faith.

WHEN MY FAMILY FRUSTRATES ME

God, I love my family members, but they frustrate me. I want to be there for them and I want them to be there for me. But they make choices I don't understand. Instead of confronting them in anger, teach me how to pray for them and speak to them with Your love. Like me, they are still growing in their relationship with You and in their knowledge of Your Word. When conflicts arise, show me how to find solutions that benefit all of us according to Your purpose and Your plan for our family.

FOR STABILITY IN RELATIONSHIPS

Lord, I ask for You to stabilize my family relationships. Help us to overcome the things that cause us to push one another away. Teach us to be steady and strong for one another. Show us how we can honor one another. Soften our hearts and help us to forgive if we feel we've been wronged.

THREE STEPS TO GOOD SPEECH

Everyone should be quick to listen,
slow to speak and slow to become angry.
JAMES 1:19

Help me with all these steps, Lord. Step number one: I need to work on my listening skills. Too often I find myself thinking of a response instead of listening to what my children are saying, and then I am rushing in with a comment or advice before they're even finished talking. Help me to sit, listen, and wait. Step number two: Remind me to pray before I speak. I need to be patient, not letting my mouth run ahead of You. And step number three: Take away my anger. That is not of You. Calm my spirit. Give me a cool head, Your thoughts, and wise words.

KIDS' TRASH TALK

There is a generation that curses its father,
and does not bless its mother.
PROVERBS 30:11 NKJV

Lord, the things my kids are saying these days! I don't know how to handle this situation. My children's words are cutting to both me and their father. Give me the right words to say to curb this kind of trash talk. The babies that I once held in my arms are growing up and I want them to grow up in You, to know You, to love You, and to follow You. To do that I desperately need Your help. Give me the wisdom I need to guide my children to You through thought, word, and deed.

HONORING OTHERS WITH MY MOUTH

Don't try to impress others. Be humble,
thinking of others as better than yourselves.
PHILIPPIANS 2:3 NLT

I don't need fancy words to impress others. I only need words guided by the mind of Christ. Help me, Lord, to honor others with my speech. I want to lift people up, not bring them down. I want to bring joy to the hearts of others, not sorrow. Give me a better attitude, positive words, and encouraging remarks. Guard my mouth and, when necessary, put Your hand upon it to keep it shut.

MY FEARS—THE POWER OF FAITH

I was terrified the first time I drove a car in England. Suddenly, I had to put aside everything I had learned about the right and wrong sides of the road. In the United States, we drive on the right—but in that country left is right. Everything is opposite.

Feeling like the other cars were going to hit me, I drove slower than usual. That is, until my brother-in-law said firmly, "Steel your nerves and press on!" I was afraid but I did what he said, praying silently, "Lord, help me do this." Finally, we completed a safe trip to our destination, and I felt a great sense of accomplishment. With the Lord's help, I had faced and conquered my fear.

Fear has many sources. When our safety is threatened, we are rightly afraid because we don't know what will happen. Our bodies are equipped with an inner alarm to signal "something is not right," in order to protect us from harm. But we need wisdom to discern real fear from false. If we hear an unfamiliar noise in the middle of the night, for instance, we may be afraid. But once we discover it's only the wind blowing branches against a windowpane, our minds can rest again.

The list of fears is endless. Melanie doesn't want to travel because she's afraid of flying. Sandra worries her son will be injured playing football. LaTrisha has dated one too many losers and fears being alone the rest of her life. Many people dread what other people may think of them. Some are afraid of making mistakes. From a fear of the dark to the horror of public speaking, many people live in trepidation. But it doesn't have to be that way.

When the Lord called Moses to free the Israelites from the slavery of Egypt, the former shepherd was very much afraid. Moses felt totally unqualified for the job, but God said to him, "I have raised you up for this very purpose, *that I might show you my power* and that my name might be proclaimed in all the earth" (Exodus 9:16, emphasis added). When we fear we're not good enough, we are looking only at our own limited abilities—instead of God's unlimited power and resources.

Praying effective prayers over our fears begins as we release those fears to God and ask Him for a heart of faith. What brings us to that point? Trust. Faith and trust overcome fear when we discover the depth of God's heart of love—and believe that He is not only capable, but more than willing, to help us in our times of need. As the apostle Paul wrote, "I know whom I have believed, and am convinced that he is able to guard what I have entrusted to him for that day" (2 Timothy 1:12).

NO DOUBT

But when he asks, he must believe and not doubt, because he who doubts is like a wave of the sea, blown and tossed by the wind.
JAMES 1:6

Lord, rescue me from my sea of doubt and fear. I have lived with uncertainty and suspicion for too long. I don't want to be like an ocean wave that is blown and tossed by the wind. I ask that You would quiet my stormy emotions and help me believe that You will take care of me. When I'm tempted to be cynical, help me choose to step away from fear and closer to faith.

SAFE IN DANGER

For in the day of trouble he will keep me safe in his dwelling; he will hide me in the shelter of his tabernacle and set me high upon a rock.
PSALM 27:5

Lord, I need Your protection. Keep me safe in your dwelling place. Hide me from my enemies in your secure shelter. Comfort me with Your warm blanket of peace and love. I am safe with You, and in Your protection—in Your presence—I can move from fearful to fearless, from timid to trusting. Here, Lord, I am safe from harm.

TRUSTING GOD WITH CHANGES

Every day I feel the tug of transition. I know change enables me to grow and become who You created me to be. Help me to be willing to step out of my comfort zone to go where You want me to be. I want to remain focused on Your purpose for me, never looking back but pressing forward in my journey with You. Show me how to lean on You when I feel out of place or alone. I know You are always with me.

TRUSTING GOD FOR SAFETY

Father, I follow hard after You. I will not be distracted but choose to be at the right place at the right time, every time. Thank You for keeping me safe today. I am secure because You have made Your angels responsible to protect me at all times. Disasters are far from me because I walk on the path of safety.

NEVER ALONE

"I will never leave you nor forsake you."
JOSHUA 1:5

Your Word says that You will never leave me, but right now I feel all alone. I am afraid of what lies before me. Help me to know, beyond a shadow of a doubt, that You are with me. You are my Good Shepherd. With You by my side, I need not fear. Fill me with Your presence and Your courage as I greet this day.

A PRAYER FOR DELIVERANCE

I sought the LORD, and He heard me,
and delivered me from all my fears.
PSALM 34:4 NKJV

I am here seeking You, Lord. I am looking in Your Word for courage and strength. Help me to have more confidence in You. You are my rock and my refuge. Bring me up to where You are. I want to commune with You, to rest with You, to be head over heels "in trust" with You. Show me how to do that, Lord. As I look upon Your face, deliver me from this burden of fear. I long to dwell in Your presence here and now, and when I rise from this place of prayer, I long to take You with me through my day. You are my courage and my strength. Nothing can harm me.

WORLDLY FEARS

"But blessed is the man who trusts in
the LORD, whose confidence is in him."
JEREMIAH 17:7

I am so blessed, for even though I fear many things right now—the state of the economy, unemployment, terrorist attacks, shootings in the schools and on the streets, lack of health care coverage—I trust in You. I refuse to go along with the world, driven by despair, fear, and insecurity. No, I will not bow to outside pressures. I will live my life with the assurance that You are with me. I will put my confidence in You, for I trust You to look out for me, to keep me close to You, to always be with me, no matter what.

TRUSTING GOD FOR STABILITY

God, I've done everything I can to make things right, and now I am doing what I should have done first—I'm letting go! Do what You will with everything I've held so tightly to. I don't need to be in control. I give it all to You now. Help me to leave it with You and not pick it back up. I'll do only what You ask me to do—nothing more.

PEACE FOR TODAY

Jesus, thank You for the peace that You give me daily. Because You have promised me peace, I refuse to be worried about things I don't have answers for right now. You know what I need to know. Thank You for the Holy Spirit You have given to encourage and guide me. He makes the hidden things known when I need to know them. I rely on Him to teach me all things and remind me of the promises in God's Word. You know what my future holds (John 14:26–29).

CALM MY HEART

God has not given us a spirit of timidity,
but of power and love and discipline.
2 TIMOTHY 1:7 NASB

Lord, rid me of the fears that are plaguing me as I come to You this morning. Calm my racing heart. Fill me with Your strength and courage. The storms, the trials, feel as if they are going to overcome me, but You have overcome the world and will not let me be brought down. You have given me the spirit of power, love, and self-discipline, and I revel in this knowledge. I praise Your name, Your saving name!

NO ONE CAN HARM ME

*So we say with confidence, "The Lord is my helper;
I will not be afraid. What can man do to me?"*
HEBREWS 13:6

Wow! I claim this promise for myself today, Lord. I commit it to
memory. You are my helper and I will not be afraid—of anything!
You are my helper, my rock, my refuge. You'll shield me from
any and all troubles this world can throw at me. I feel You sitting
beside me, Your hands upon mine. Nothing can harm me with You
by my side. How awesome is that! Today, I arise with confidence,
telling the whole world, "The Lord is my helper! I am not afraid!"

LEANING ON THE WORD

*For you have been my hope, O Sovereign LORD,
my confidence since my youth.*
PSALM 71:5

Lord, since I've known You, You have been my hope—most
times my only hope. You give me confidence to face the day.
Sometimes I'm afraid to step out the door, to watch the news, to
read the paper. But at those times all I need to do is remember
Your Word and trust in that. Your Word is my confidence and
my strength. When those arrows of misfortune come my way,
help me to lean back and rest in Your Word, committing Your
promises to memory, strengthening my spirit and my soul.

BREAKING FEAR'S GRIP

God, I admit that sometimes fear grips me. I want to be strong in faith, but sometimes circumstances are just too much. Help me to recognize fear and draw strength from You so I can break fear's grip when it begins to overwhelm me. Forgive me when I try to handle life on my own. I want to depend on You, but sometimes it's hard to let go. Teach me how to trust You, since I know You are more than able to deal with any circumstance I encounter.

TRUSTING GOD FOR MY FUTURE

My life is an obstacle course filled with things that try to keep me off balance. But I draw strength from You. When I pray, I know You hear me. You make plans for me to have a successful life and a prosperous future. I cannot fail because You are directing me as I look to You for guidance. Thank You, Lord, that no matter how many times I fall, You always reach down to take my hand and help me up again.

NO FEAR IN LOVE

There is no fear in love. But perfect love drives out fear,
because fear has to do with punishment. The one
who fears is not made perfect in love.
1 JOHN 4:18

Lord, I thank You that Your great love conquers fear! I can love people freely because You live in me. It doesn't have to be scary to reveal my inner self. I don't have to fear rejection. I may be accepted or not, but either way I can love with confidence because Your perfect love drives out fear. Give me the courage to live that life of love.

GOD STRENGTHENS YOU

"So do not fear, for I am with you; do not be dismayed,
for I am your God. I will strengthen you and help you;
I will uphold you with my righteous right hand."
ISAIAH 41:10

Lord, I need Your strength in me. Stronger than steel, your character is so solid I don't have to be afraid. You are with me—and that means everything. I can have joy because of Your joy in me. With Your righteous right hand you help me, deliver me, and uphold me. As You take my hand and say, "Do not fear, I will help you," I smile in gratitude and thanks.

MY FINANCES—THE POWER OF WISE STEWARDSHIP

Diane loves to shop. She jokes that she was born with a credit card in hand—and she uses it freely at the mall. Her husband, Ben, is just the opposite. He won't buy anything unless it's on sale, and he painstakingly accounts for every penny he spends. Ben and Diane love God and each other, but they fight constantly over money issues.

Whether we are married, single, widowed, or divorced, whether we're a tightwad or a spendthrift, each of us has a need to pray powerfully for financial wisdom. If God is able to mend our broken bones and shattered hearts—and He is—He's also capable of fixing our finances.

God's Word has much to teach us about money and finance—in fact, there are well over two thousand verses in the Bible that refer to the topic of money. Clearly, our handling of money—our stewardship—is important to God, and requires us to persevere in our prayer lives. God always answers our prayers. Sometimes He does so in ways that are quite unexpected.

When Sue was accepted to graduate school, she began to doubt whether she could really afford it. Sue prayed, saying, "God, if this is really what You want for me, then I need a sign. I think I need five thousand dollars." A few days later she received a check in the mail for exactly that amount. It was from her grandfather, who said he felt strongly led to send her money, in that amount, in that particular week. Now, whenever doubts arise in other areas of her life, Sue remembers God's faithfulness through this blessing.

God allows some to receive help and others to give it. Lydia was a wealthy woman whom God used for His good purposes. A "seller of purple" in Philippi, she heard the apostle Paul's message of Jesus Christ and responded. Lydia and her household were baptized, and she generously opened her home to Paul and his companions (Acts 16:14–15).

As we read key verses on financial topics, we become well equipped to pray targeted prayers that will help us control our spending, save for the future, get out of debt, and find contentment and balance. The power of prayer makes us generous givers and changes our attitude toward things. As we spend time praising God, we worry less and trust God more.

BIBLICAL PERSPECTIVE ON MONEY

*Now it is required that those who have
been given a trust must prove faithful.*
1 CORINTHIANS 4:2

Lord, I am thankful for the financial resources with which You
have blessed me. I want to be a good steward, a wise manager,
of the resources You have entrusted to me. Help me to save and
spend with discernment and give to others in need. Help me to
find balance—not be a hoarder or an out-of-control spender.
Give me a godly view of money and how to use it in ways that
will honor You.

SPENDING WISELY

*For the love of money is a root of all kinds of evil.
Some people, eager for money, have wandered from
the faith and pierced themselves with many griefs.*
1 TIMOTHY 6:10

Lord, You are the one who gives wisdom—and I ask that you
would give me the discernment I need to spend money sensibly.
I need money to pay my bills and meet my obligations. I know
from Your Word that money itself is not evil; it's the love of
money—greed—that makes us wander from the faith. Help me
to spend the money You provide not in self-indulgence but in
good judgment.

LEARNED CONTENTMENT

Lord, I am so happy just as I am. There is nothing better than being in Your presence, seeking Your face. I thank You for all my blessings, in good times and bad. I thank You for Your Son, who died on the cross so that I could live forever. I thank You for Your Word and the treasures I find there. I go forth in this day, with the power of contentment firmly in my heart. Lead me where You will. I am ready to follow.

STRENGTH FOR THE WORK AHEAD

You promised to bless me and mine. I thank You for all the spiritual, physical, and financial gifts You have showered upon me. You give me the physical strength to go out each and every day to work and support myself and my family. Your Word gives me the spiritual strength to battle the schemes that the evil one throws into my path. Thank You for hearing my prayers, morning after morning, strengthening me for the work ahead.

LOVE OF MONEY

Dear God, I come to You this morning with a heavy heart. I feel as if I have let my quest for financial security take my eyes off of You. Help me to put aside my fear of never having enough and replace it with trust in You. Take away my seemingly insatiable appetite for more and more gain and replace it with the power of contentment. Free me from the snare of greed and lead me into greater faith in You.

HOPEFUL IN GOD, RICH IN GENEROSITY

I am setting my hope on You this morning, Lord, for You provide me with everything to enjoy. Your treasures of creation—trees, flowers, children, animals, sunsets, stars—are wonders to my eyes and a balm to my heart. With You supplying all that I need, I can do good works, be ready to share, and thus build up treasures in heaven. This way of life, enveloped by the presence of the living God, is the true way. Keep my feet sure on this path. Take care of me through this day and the days to come.

SAVING AND INVESTING

In the house of the wise are stores of choice food and oil,
but a foolish man devours all he has.
PROVERBS 21:20

Lord, I pray that You would lead me to wise financial advice. When I look, help me to find a trusted source who can give me direction as to where to best save and invest my resources. Please provide for my needs today and help me to save for the future. Help me to be responsible with my finances as I trust You as my Provider.

JOY IN GIVING

Each man should give what he has decided in his heart to give, not
reluctantly or under compulsion, for God loves a cheerful giver.
2 CORINTHIANS 9:7

Lord, I thank You for Your blessings. Whether in plenty or with little, I want to be a cheerful giver. I desire to give from a full heart that serves joyfully, not reluctantly or with complaining. I long to see Your money used in ways that will bless others—through my tithing at church, giving to mission organizations, or helping the needy. I choose to give at whatever level I can—and ask You to bless it.

GOD WILL PROVIDE

*"Therefore I tell you, do not worry about your life, what
you will eat or drink; or about your body, what you will wear.
Is not life more important than food, and the body more important
than clothes? Look at the birds of the air; they do not sow or reap
or store away in barns, and yet your heavenly Father feeds them.
Are you not much more valuable than they? Who of you
by worrying can add a single hour to his life?"*
MATTHEW 6:25–27

Lord, I thank You for providing for my needs. I give You my
worries and fears—those nagging thoughts about lacking money
for clothes, food, and the basics of life. You feed the sparrows in the
field, Lord—You'll certainly help me and my family. Your resources
are limitless—You have an abundance of blessings. I praise You for
Your goodness, Lord, and the faithfulness of Your provision.

THE RIGHT HEART-SET

A heart-set is like a mind-set, Lord. Each morning I need to ask myself where my heart is. Is it set on making lots of money so that I can buy things I don't really need? Is my heart set on showing how much better off I am than my neighbor? Rather, I pray that my heart is set on You and what You want me to do each and every moment of the day. Help me not get caught up in this "me" world. I want my life to be all about You.

DE-ACCUMULATING

I want to be perfect and mature in You, Christ. I'm not sure it would be a good idea right now to sell all that I have, and I'm not sure that's what You'd want. But there are things I have that I could donate to those in need. Help me not to give away the worst that I own but the best to those needing food, shelter, and clothing. Help me to choose wisely as I give to others and follow You who had nothing in this world, not even a place to lay Your head, yet owned it all!

MY FRIENDS—THE POWER OF CONNECTION

What would we do without friends? They encourage and inspire us. They listen like they really care—because they do. Good friends seek to understand and empathize with us. Even when they can't relate, they care about us anyway.

Friends are fun! We enjoy being around them. When we can talk, laugh, pray, and play with someone we trust, have found a real treasure. We give and receive, we love and learn. Above all, in friendship, we seek what is best for each other. No matter what our age or life stage, we never outgrow our need for connection, for having and being a good friend.

Loving with words and actions is a hallmark of true friendship. I remember once being stressed for weeks about an important deadline at work. The project weighed heavily on me, so I had been living on snacks instead of using my precious time to grocery shop. On top of it all, I was getting a sore throat. When my friend Maria learned I was taking ill, she promptly came with four bags of groceries from the health-food store— and prayed for me to stay well. I was astonished at her thoughtful generosity. And I soon began to feel better.

Like snowflakes, no two friendships are the same; each brings a unique beauty and joy to our lives. We have acquaintances, casual friends, close friends, and "heart" friends, that handful of individuals with whom we share our deepest selves. Jesus had different circles of friends, too. He ministered to the crowds, He spent significant time with the twelve disciples, and He was closest to three men: Peter, James, and John. He was a companion to tax collectors and sinners (Mark 2:15–17), as well as His dearly loved friends Mary, Martha, and Lazarus (John 11:20–32).

Today, each of us can have the joy of knowing Jesus as our friend (John 15:15). In the quiet solitude of prayer we can pour out our deepest fears and desires. We can take pleasure in enjoying God—of just being in His company. "Fellowship with Him [Jesus] is a matter of priorities, and a matter of choice," says Ken Gire in *Intimate Moments with the Savior*. "It's the better part of the meal life has to offer. It is, in fact, the main course."

When we fellowship with God in prayer, we can then pray powerfully for our earthly friends. We can pray *for* them and *with* them in Jesus' name.

That's perhaps one of the best ways we can show a friend we care. Maybe someone we know is going through a separation or divorce and could use a phone call. Perhaps a new neighbor, a recent widow, or a new mom may need the unexpected blessing of friendly kindness. Maybe we should stop to thank God for the wonderful women in our lives—those who've given us the gift of friendship—and ask Him how we can be a better friend to others.

THANK YOU FOR MY FRIENDSHIPS

A man of many companions may come to ruin,
but there is a friend who sticks closer than a brother.
PROVERBS 18:24

Lord, I thank You for my wonderful friends! As I think about the treasure chest of my close friends, casual friends, and acquaintances, I am grateful for the blessings and the joys each one brings to my life. Thank You for my "heart friends," my loyal sister friends who listen, care, and encourage me. They are my faithful companions. I acknowledge that You, Lord, are the giver of all good gifts, and I thank You for Your provision in friendships.

FRIENDS HELP EACH OTHER

If one falls down, his friend can help him up.
But pity the man who falls and has no one to help him up!
ECCLESIASTES 4:10

Lord, sometimes it's easier to give than to receive. I want to be a giver, to take the time to care and help my friends when they need it. And help me to learn to receive, too—so that I'm not too proud to receive generosity from a friend. Give and take, Lord...we really do need each other.

BEING A BETTER LISTENER

Come and listen, all you who fear God;
let me tell you what he has done for me.
PSALM 66:16

Lord, I praise You today for all You have done for me. You have brought help, hope, healing, and restoration, and I want to tell people! Help me proclaim Your goodness, sharing the amazing ways You have come through for me. But as I speak, help me to be a good listener, too. Through Your spirit, Lord, may I show I care about my friends. Give me wisdom to know when my ears should be open and my mouth shut.

CHOOSING FRIENDS WISELY

Your Word says two are better than one, because if one falls, there will be someone to lift that person up. Lord, I ask for divine connections, good friends only You can give. Help me to let go of relationships that are unhealthy and negative. I want friends who speak and live positively, who inspire and encourage but also tell me the truth when I need to hear it. Give me wisdom today in the relationships I choose.

TO BE A BETTER FRIEND

Father, help me to be sensitive to the people around me. When I am tempted to make things all about me, remind me that You created me for friendship. I want to be a better friend. Help me to prefer others to myself. I want to be a better listener so I really hear my friends. I want to help them if I can in the things that concern them. Let my words encourage them. Show me how to strengthen them with Your goodness.

RESTORING A BROKEN FRIENDSHIP

Above all, love each other deeply,
because love covers over a multitude of sins.
1 PETER 4:8

Lord, I thank You for Your healing balm that covers the hurt and pain I've experienced in this friendship. Your grace covers me; Your love repairs my brokenness, and You give me the ability to love again. Help me to put aside the wounds of my heart and to be a friend again. I thank You and praise You that Your love is healing and restoring. Thank You, Lord, for putting this friendship back together again.

LOYALTY

"Is this your loyalty to your friend?
Why did you not go with your friend?"
2 SAMUEL 16:17 NASB

Lord, I want to be a better friend to those I love. Help me
to be trustworthy, devoted, and reliable. Help me to put the
desires of my friends before my own. Give me the power of
encouragement, so that I may be at their sides with a ready
word and a shoulder to lean on, with love in my heart and a
prayer on my lips. I want to be like Jonathan was for David. I
want to clothe others with the warmth of friendship. Make me
a true friend. Whom can I help today?

LOVE ONE ANOTHER

[Jesus said,] "Love one another; as I have loved you."
JOHN 13:34 NKJV

What an example of love You give us, Jesus! You laid down Your
life for everyone—even while we were still sinners. Fill me with
that kind of love, Lord, that self-sacrificing love. So often my
thoughts seem to be all about me and what I want. Help me to
change that by following Your example. I want to be like You,
serving others with compassion, understanding, patience, and
kindness. Give me that power, that longing, to love those who
love me, those who hate me, and those who are indifferent to me.

TURNING THE OTHER CHEEK

The Lord restored the fortunes of Job when he prayed for his friends,
and the Lord increased all that Job had twofold.
JOB 42:10 NASB

Job prayed for his friends even though they had argued with
him and showed him their true colors. That's a true friend, Lord.
And when he did this, You blessed him, giving him twice as
much as he had before. That's amazing! That's the true power of
forgiveness. You know the relationships I have with my friends.
Sometimes it's hard to overlook the hurtful things they say and
do. Help me to be more like Job—to learn to turn the other
cheek and actually serve friends who disappoint me. I come
to You this morning asking for that kind of compassion and
dedication to my friends, Lord.

BLESSED WITH FRIENDS

The sweet smell of perfume and oils is pleasant,
and so is good advice from a friend.
PROVERBS 27:9 NCV

There are many wonderful things in this life, Lord. The smell of a baby's breath, the touch of a warm hand, the taste of dark chocolate—but a good word, deed, or thought from a friend is even better. There are times when I am so down. And then a friend blesses me and I think of You. It's You and the love that You give that makes us want to reach out to others. Thank You for blessing my life with friends.

NEW FRIENDS

If one falls down, the other can help him up. But it is bad for the
person who is alone and falls, because no one is there to help.
ECCLESIASTES 4:10 NCV

Lord, there are people out there who are hard to love. Help me to look beyond their cold demeanor, rudeness, shyness, negative words, and bad attitudes. You love each and every one of us and want us all to be friends. And if we were friends even to our enemies, the world would be at peace at last. No one deserves to be alone. Give me the courage and strength to reach out to all people and to make new friends.

WORDS OF ENCOURAGEMENT

What You do for me each and every day is amazing. What You have done for me in the past is incomprehensible. Thank You for Your Word that shows me how great a friend You are to me and how I can be a good friend to others as well. There is nothing as powerful as Your Word for direction and encouragement. This morning, this day, plant Your Word—the elixir of life—in my heart. Mold it into my spirit. Help me to claim it in my own life and then share it with others.

SERVANT LOVE

O Lord, I want to do whatever my friends desire, as long as it is in accordance with Your Word. May I have the same attitude with my friends as Jonathan had with David. He served him so well, doing whatever David's soul desired. That is servant love, the kind You continually show us. Help me to be a better friend. Let me know what to say, when to speak, and whom to encourage. I want to do Your will in the world. Lead me on!

A FIRMLY FOUNDED FRIENDSHIP

I want to do what it takes to build lasting friendships with people You have put in my life, Lord. My friends are important to me. Yet life is busy, and sometimes I put the things I need to do to get ahead before my relationships. Lord, help me to establish a firm foundation of loyalty, trust, honesty, and integrity in my friendships. When our eyes are on You, we will remain strong in our commitment to You and to one another. Help me to discern when I need to drop a task and be there for my friends.

TRUTHFUL FRIENDSHIP

The Bible says that as iron sharpens iron, so true friends sharpen the hearts and minds of one another. God, I want to have relationships that are true and honest. Help me to tell the truth in the gentlest and most positive way. I want my friends to know the truth about me and about the things that concern them. When they ask my advice, help me to share truth and wisdom from You that will help them grow in their relationship with You. Show them that I love them and want Your best for their lives.

MY FUTURE—THE POWER OF PURSUING GOD'S PLAN

Do family and friends look at you as if you should have a plan for the rest of your life? It can be overwhelming when people ask you to present them with the complete blueprint for your future. The truth is, all of us feel lost at times. A comedian once said, "The reason why adults ask children what they want to be when they grow up is because they're looking for suggestions!" It's okay to admit you don't have all the answers.

God created you to succeed. We can get so busy pursuing our futures that we can forget that His ways are higher than our ways. Jeremiah 29:11 says, "'For I know the plans I have for you,' declares the LORD, 'plans to prosper you and not to harm you, plans to give you hope and a future.'" We're all guilty of coming up with our own plans, putting them into action, and then hoping and praying that God will bless them.

We all have great plans for our futures. And since God doesn't give us a personal course description laid out word for word for the rest of our lives, we can be tempted to go our own ways. *My way or God's way?* It makes sense that the Creator of the universe would have the ultimate plan for our lives; yet we often struggle for control. Frankly, it's a scary feeling to relinquish total control of our lives to a Being we can't see or touch. Faith requires that we live one day at a time following His lead.

At first glance you might think David had it made as a young man. After all, he knew his future—God said he would be the next king of Israel. Although his own family never considered him a candidate, God promised him the throne.

David's story begins in 1 Samuel 16 when he is called in

from tending his father's sheep and anointed as the next king of Israel. His future probably didn't play out like he imagined—he didn't go from the sheep pasture immediately to the throne. He had to hold tightly to the promise God had given him. It took many years, and David experienced failures alongside great victories before he ever wore his crown.

No doubt David asked God the same questions you've asked: *When? Why? How? Are You still there? Is this still Your will for my life?* The prayers and cries of David's heart are recorded in many of the psalms as he pursued God's plan for his future.

Maybe, like David, you know what you want to do with your life. Perhaps you've had a passion for something since you were a child, but now as a graduate you're finding that God's plan looks different from yours.

God is always faithful to lead and guide you. God has set your course, and it's okay if you don't know every single detail of His plan. Take time to pray and follow His directions one day at a time.

WAITING ON THE FUTURE

Just as You promised David that he would be king, You have made promises to me for my life. I know everything You promised will happen, and I'm excited about the future. It's hard to wait on the future I know You have planned for me. Help me to find patience to be content doing what I should be doing now while on my way to achieving the purpose You have for my life.

Know also that wisdom is sweet to your soul; if you find it, there is a future hope for you, and your hope will not be cut off.
PROVERBS 24:14

REVEALING OF GOD'S PLAN

Father, You have placed Your purposes deep within my heart. When I look inside myself now, help me see only what You have planned for me. Give me courage to step out with confidence, knowing that You perfect everything that concerns me.

LOVED NOW AND FOREVER

I am convinced that neither death nor life, neither angels nor demons,
neither the present nor the future, nor any powers, neither height nor
depth, nor anything else in all creation, will be able to separate us
from the love of God that is in Christ Jesus our Lord.
ROMANS 8:38–39

No matter what happens, Lord, I cannot be separated from You and Your love. Oh, what that means to me! Fill me with the love that never ends. May it flow through me and reach those I meet this day. May my future be filled with blessing upon blessing, and may I praise You today and in the days to come.

A FUTURE FOR ME

Consider the blameless, observe the upright;
there is a future for the man of peace.
PSALM 37:37

Lord, I am Your child, a child of peace. When someone strikes me on the left cheek, I turn my head and give them the other. I can only do this through Your power. Nothing can harm me when I am living so close to You. Now, with the next breath I take, give me the gift of stillness, of silence, as I put my future, my hopes, my dreams into Your capable hands.

NO FEAR FOR THE FUTURE

Do not allow my foot to stumble, Lord. Eliminate the obstacles of worry and fear that line the path before me. Give me hope and courage to face my future. Give me a clear mind to make the right decisions. And at the end of this day, give me the peace of sweet slumber as I lie down within Your mighty arms.

UNKNOWN FUTURE

Indeed, how can people avoid what
they don't know is going to happen?
ECCLESIASTES 8:7 NLT

Dear God, I don't know what lies before me. I feel plagued by the what-ifs that tumble through my mind and pierce my confident spirit. Allow me to let You fill my soul. Help me to be confident in Your wisdom and power to guide me, so that, although You have concealed from me the knowledge of future events, I may be ready for any changes that arise.

GIVING GOD CONTROL OF MY FUTURE

Jesus, You knew that God's will was for You to give Your life so that others may experience God. You gave God total control and submitted to His will. Help me to do the same. I was created for a specific purpose. You have a plan for my life, and I want to complete everything You created me to accomplish. Help me to live my life according to Your ultimate plan.

> *People may make plans in their minds,*
> *but the LORD decides what they will do.*
> PROVERBS 16:9 NCV

PRAYER OF DISCERNMENT

That same Spirit who raised Christ from the dead lives in me. Thank You that my heart is sensitive to Your purposes and plans for my life. I clearly distinguish between right and wrong; I see the light and walk in it. I trust You, Lord, with all my heart and refuse to rely on my own understanding in any matter. Help me to choose Your way, the right way, every time. I am determined to know You and discern Your voice when You're speaking to me, just as a child knows the voice of a parent.

GOD'S PLAN OF BLESSING

The Bible tells me that whatever I put my hand to will prosper. I am blessed in the city and in the field, when I come into my house, and when I go out of it. Your blessing on my life provides for my every need. I ask for Your wisdom, Lord. Teach me to make the right choices and decisions for my life. You make me a blessing because I belong to You.

> *"I am the LORD your God, who teaches you to profit,*
> *who leads you in the way you should go."*
> ISAIAH 48:17 NASB

WALKING TOWARD YOUR DESTINY

Sometimes my life feels upside down, and I need You to come along and flip it right side up. Point me in the right direction; place me directly on Your path for my life. Please don't let me miss a beat. Help me to be willing always to walk with You toward my destiny. When I become distracted or make a wrong turn, sound the alarm of my heart and I will run to You. Set my feet back on the right course and keep me moving in the right direction.

GOD'S PLANS

But the plans of the LORD stand firm forever,
the purposes of his heart through all generations.
PSALM 33:11

You have led me to this place where I now lie before You, seeking
Your presence and Your face, Your guidance and Your strength.
Your plans for my life stand firm, although they are as yet
unrevealed to me. With one glance, You see all the generations
that have gone before, that are present now, and that will come in
the future. You see it all! Allow me to rest in the knowledge that
each and every day You go before me, and that in the end, all will
be well with my soul.

OUR PLANS, GOD'S PURPOSE

People can make all kinds of plans,
but only the LORD's plan will happen.
PROVERBS 19:21 NCV

You know the plans of my mind and the desires of my heart, but
as Your Word says, it is Your purpose that will rule the day. Help
me to step aside if I am blocking Your way. Help me to keep
confident in Your Word and in Your plan for my life. I await Your
instructions for the day.

LOOKING FORWARD

Sometimes I look back at the things that didn't turn out quite right for me. I know I shouldn't focus on wrongs done to me or opportunities missed. You have set a great life before me, and I want to embrace it without the shadow of the past. Help me see the future with joy and expectation. My hope is in *You*!

> *"When the Spirit of truth comes, he will guide you into all truth. He will not speak on his own but will tell you what he has heard. He will tell you about the future."*
> JOHN 16:13 NLT

FUTURE SUCCESS

The Bible encourages me to store my treasures in heaven, and I want to do that, but You have also promised me success here on earth. Today I ask You for wisdom in everything I do. Help me to live my life with honor and integrity so I can bring glory to Your name. Teach me Your ways so I continually walk in Your blessings. Thank You for causing others to respect me because I am a reflection of You. I pray others see something in me that sets me apart and points them to You.

THE POWER OF RECOGNIZING SEASONS

Father, I know there is a season for everything. I was born at the right season, and this is my time to live a great life. The Bible tells me there is a time for every purpose under heaven—a time to weep, a time to laugh, a time to mourn, and a time to dance. Help me to recognize the season I am in and to flow with it. I don't want to be resistant. Show me how to bend with Your leading.

> *To everything there is a season,*
> *a time for every purpose under heaven.*
> ECCLESIASTES 3:1 NKJV

PLANNING AHEAD

You know my life gets so busy that I seem to get stuck in the moment. Remind me to lift up my head and look to the future. Help me to have realistic and attainable goals. Show me how to balance my life for today while at the same time planning for tomorrow. Remind me to set my eyes on You so I can see where we're going together, with my future on the horizon.

> *The ants are not a strong people,*
> *but they prepare their food in the summer.*
> PROVERBS 30:25 NASB

MY HABITS—THE POWER OF A HEALTHY LIFESTYLE

Everyone has habits—good and bad. Habits are behaviors you do without thinking about them. They are like simple math: they either add to your life or subtract from it. Do you know people who push everything to the last minute? Procrastinating subtracts from their lives. It robs them of success at work, in relationships, and in achieving their goals, no matter how small.

What about someone who can't hold on to money? No matter how much money they make, it seems to burn a hole in their pocket, and they never have enough. It goes out as fast as it comes in. That habit of spending subtracts from living a healthy financial life.

Then there are those who are committed to adding to their lives. Consider the person who demonstrates healthy discipline by eating right and exercising. We know people who pray and feed their spirits regularly. They are growing in their walks with the Lord, and they exhibit spiritual strength.

The power of living a healthy life is determined by the positive and negative habits you establish. To achieve your goals, you need to eliminate habits that would take away from your success and to surround yourself with the support that encourages you to add to your life.

The best way to break a bad habit is to replace it with a good one. Let's say before you became a Christ follower you partied every Saturday night. It's hard to sit at home on Saturdays and think about how much fun your old friends are having. Instead, make a commitment to do something else each Saturday night— join a small group from your church for game night or go to a

Saturday night worship service.

Breaking a bad habit is simply choosing something different. Stop doing what you've always done and do something that adds to your life. Become more aware of what you are doing and exercise control over your thoughts, feelings, and actions.

What habits are taking away from various areas of your life? Do you need to be more diligent with your time? Do you need to be a better friend? Take time right now and commit to establishing a new habit.

Ask God to help you develop an action plan that will help you replace the bad habit with a positive one. You don't have to do it alone. God will walk with you through it. Draw on His strength and consider asking someone you trust to help you be accountable. Focus on one habit at a time and work your way to a healthy lifestyle in Christ.

ADDRESSING BAD HABITS

Father, I don't want to talk to You about this habit I have, but I know I need to. It makes me want to hide from You. It keeps me from attaining my full potential, and I want to stop. I know I can stop with Your help. Help me to see the real reason for my habit and show me how to heal the pain that drives me to keep doing it. Give me the courage to keep trying if I mess up. Help me to stay strong and just say no to guilt.

FORMING A HABIT OF PRAYER

I am so thankful that I can talk to You, Lord. Time spent with You in prayer feeds my spirit and fills me with Your power and strength. I am always tempted to come to You with my list of things I want, when I should just sit and listen to what You have to say. Help me to be more diligent with my prayer time.

MAKING FORGIVENESS A HABIT

God, You always forgive me, but sometimes it's hard to forgive myself. I feel so ashamed when I continue to do things that I've committed to You and myself not to do. The Bible says that once I ask You for forgiveness, You don't remember my sin—but I do. It comes to mind day after day and brings guilt and shame with it. Cleanse my heart and mind of this guilt, Lord. Help me to forgive myself. Help me love myself in spite of my faults—the way You love me.

ADD TO YOUR FAITH

Father, You have given me great and precious promises. With these promises I can live separate from the world, removed from its evil desires. Because You have given me these blessings, I am determined to add to my faith goodness, knowledge, and self-control today. Help me to grow in patience and in service for You. Help me to show kindness and love to others. As I nurture these things in my life, help me to know You more.

MAINTAINING A HEALTHY WEIGHT

Lord, I hate to diet. Instead I want to make a lifestyle change. Give me hope to make a lasting change. I can do nothing on my own—I can only be successful when I rely on Your strength. Show me the right choices that will enable me to change. Teach me how to feed my body what it needs instead of what I want. Free me from emotional eating. Give me a new desire to exercise and live a healthy life. Please send people into my life who will encourage me in this commitment.

SELF-SPEAK

God, You know that sometimes I am not nice to myself. I say things that are negative about myself, the way I look and feel. I beat myself up over the choices I make. Teach me to talk to myself as You would. Show me what Your Word says about me. Help me to grow in self-confidence. Show me how to encourage myself in You, like David did. Teach me to talk to myself from Your perspective of who I am.

A HABIT OF LAUGHTER

Father, I haven't had a good belly laugh in a long time. I don't mean to take life too seriously. Bring times of refreshing into my life. Remind me to look for opportunities to experience the joy of laughter. Point them out to me and then help me to let go and have a good time. Laughter seems to release stress and adjust my attitude. Inject me with funny thoughts when I need to relax and have a good laugh.

WINDOWS OF MY SOUL

Lord, one image can affect my thoughts for days. Give me wisdom to protect my heart and mind from the things I should not see. Help me to avoid things that would hurt my heart.

DEVOTED TO TRUTH

Lord, when I am devoted to Your truth, it becomes clear what things do and don't belong in my life. I don't want to believe the lie that truth is relative. Show me truth in black and white. Help me to break the habits that keep me from living a life pleasing to You. As I am tempted to repeat an old habit, remind me that You are there with me, ready to help me let go. Help me to live according to Your truth.

LIFE IN YOUR WORD

God, Your Word breathes life into me. Help me to be committed to Your Word, to study it, and to place it in my heart. Bring Your words back to me as I go through my day. Instruct me, encourage me, and fill me with Your words.

A HABIT OF SELFLESSNESS

Lord, I've been self-centered. There have been times when I felt like the world revolved around me. Forgive me for such selfishness. I won't die if everything doesn't go my way. Help me not to react so emotionally when something doesn't turn out as I expected. Give me compassion for others and a sense of selflessness to serve them.

> *Since Christ suffered while he was in his body, strengthen*
> *yourselves with the same way of thinking Christ had.*
> *The person who has suffered in the body is finished with sin.*
> 1 PETER 4:1 NCV

STOPPING PROCRASTINATION

Jesus, I've been so bad at putting things off until the last minute. Forgive me! Help me to do the things I should. I want to be ahead instead of behind. Help me to order my day right and to make it a habit to tackle the most obnoxious task first and get it done. When I have the thought, *I'll do it later*, help me to use that thought as a cue that I'm procrastinating. Then give me strength to act fast and do my task right then.

RELATIONSHIP HABITS

Father, I have a bad habit of needing others to pay attention to me. I want them to notice and speak to me. My confidence should come from knowing You and believing I will become who You created me to be. I don't need the approval of others, especially those I don't know. Speak to me when I do this. Help me to stop. Show me how to turn my focus from myself to them. I can't show Your love to others if I'm seeking something from them. Help me to establish good relationship habits.

THE POWER TO CHANGE

Help me, Lord, to focus on the positive qualities that I have and the Word of God that describes me in the light of Your love. I am an overcomer in Christ Jesus. I am a new creature in Christ, with new thoughts, intents, and purposes. My mind is made new as I spend time with You. Remind me of just how much You love me. I rely on Your strength to help me to make the changes I need to make today.

ACCEPTING RESPONSIBILITY FOR MY ACTIONS

It would be easier to deny my mistakes to myself and to others, but I want to be a person of integrity and honor. Truth is important to You—and to me. Lord, give me the courage to take responsibility for my actions. I know that with each action there are consequences, both positive and negative. Help me to think before I act and to listen to Your instruction and direction for decisions I make, no matter how big or small.

ACCEPTING RESPONSIBILITY FOR MY WORDS

My words are powerful—they can add to or take away from someone's life. I want to be a positive influence in the lives of those around me. I want to encourage them with Your goodness and love. I want to be truthful, and sometimes it's hard to say certain things, but I'm asking You to help me speak the truth in love. For those I have hurt with my words, help me to take responsibility, apologize, and set things right with them. Lord, put a guard over my mouth so I speak Your words in love.

MY HEALTH—
THE POWER OF HEALING AND RESTORATION

Health is one of our greatest God-given assets. "The healthier we are, the more stable our emotions," says Joyce Meyer in *Look Great, Feel Great*. "A healthy person can handle disappointments easier than one who is unhealthy. They can remain stable through the storms of life." But though many of us understand that our bodies are temples (1 Corinthians 6:19), we often treat them more like trash cans. Are we really taking care of ourselves when we eat junk food, avoid exercise, and fill our minds with the negativity of today's entertainment?

We can pray powerful and effective prayers for health, healing, and wholeness, in our lives and in the lives of others, when we

- *pray boldly:* "Let us then approach the throne of grace with confidence, so that we may receive mercy and find grace to help us in our time of need" (Hebrews 4:16);
- *ask in Jesus' name:* "Until now you have not asked for anything in my name. Ask and you will receive, and your joy will be complete" (John 16:24);
- *pray in faith:* "If you believe, you will receive whatever you ask for in prayer" (Matthew 21:22).

Faith and prayer go together. Martin Luther said, "Faith makes the prayer acceptable because it believes that either the prayer will be answered, or that something better will be given instead."

When we pray, we release the power of heaven into our lives. But there are times when our prayers for healing are not answered with a yes. How do we cope—and what can we learn? In his classic book *Prayer*, George A. Buttrick says, "True prayer does not evade pain, but gains from it insight, patience, courage, and sympathy. . . . This is healing beyond healing. By this prayer we are 'more than conquerors': the realism of unanswered prayer becomes the very Presence of God."

Mary Ann provides a good example of this. Diagnosed with multiple sclerosis at age twenty-seven, she was soon debilitated—but then, surprisingly, the disease went into remission for several years. When her daughter left for college, Mary Ann's health quickly declined again, and she was confined to a wheelchair for the rest of her life.

Early on, Mary Ann had prayed, "God, please let me be well enough to raise my girls." It was by His grace that her disease was in remission all the years her children were growing up. Mary Ann's daughter marvels at the fact that her mother never complained about the unfairness of MS—she accepted the life God gave her and used the resources she had to beautifully represent her Lord. When Mary Ann died at age sixty-five, scores of people attended a memorial service to give thanks for her encouraging example.

When God heals, we praise Him. When He does not, we praise Him still. Either way, we are changed within.

FOR GOOD HEALTH

Say to him: "Long life to you! Good health to you and
your household! And good health to all that is yours!"
1 SAMUEL 25:6

Lord, I thank You for my good health. It is a blessing. I pray for
Your power to sustain me as I take care of myself—by eating
healthy food, drinking enough water, and making movement
and exercise a part of my daily life. Give me the self-control and
motivation I need to make wise choices to support the health of
my mind, my spirit, and my body. Please keep me from injury
and illness, and keep me safe, I pray.

SPIRITUAL HEALTH

Lord, I need Your times of refreshing in my life. Bread of
Heaven, as You nourish my body with food, feed my soul with
Your words of comfort and life. May I be filled with Your healing
love, joy, and goodness. I praise You, Father, for providing green
pastures, places to relax and unwind in the Spirit. Please still my
heart from distractions and be the Restorer of my soul.

PROMISES FOR LONG LIFE

God, You have given me so many promises in the Bible. Help me to learn and keep them close to my heart. Thank You for watching over me and promising me a long life. You have given me the opportunity and ability to live according to Your Word. Forgive me when I mess up, and help me to choose life each day. Give me strength to do Your will as I choose right living. As I come to know You better, I pray that I will know with more assurance what You would have me do.

GETTING RID OF STRESS

Cast all your anxiety on him because he cares for you.
1 PETER 5:7

Lord, help me to find relief from stress in my life. I need to value rest and make time to relax—and I need Your power to do so. I cast my cares on You, my Burden Bearer. Help me to deal with the toxic, unhealthy relationships in my life. Give me the strength to say no when I need better emotional boundaries. And please help me find joy again in the things I like to do— unwinding with music, taking a walk, calling a friend, or learning a new hobby. Calm me and renew me, Lord.

WHOLENESS AND RIGHT LIVING

Do not be wise in your own eyes; fear the LORD and shun evil. This will bring health to your body and nourishment to your bones.
PROVERBS 3:7–8

Lord, help me to be a person who takes care of herself. As I look to Your wisdom for right living, may I enjoy a healthy body. I need to take responsibility for my actions—what I choose to put in my mouth and my mind is up to me. Help me to make wise decisions and to be a good steward of myself, the "temple" you have given me. Help me not to abuse my body, but to care for it as You would want me to.

CHOOSE LIFE

Jesus, You offered me life, not just life after death but eternal life that started the day I asked You to live in my heart. Help me to remember that every choice I make is a choice for life or for death, for blessing or cursing. I don't want to live one day less on the earth because of a poor choice I made. Help me to make every decision count.

A HEALTHY SOUL

God, my thoughts affect my mind, will, and emotions. When I'm spending too much time thinking about negative things, wake me up. Help me to let go of the thoughts that bring me down. Remind me to think of all that is pure and right. I can't change the past, and it doesn't help to worry about the future. Help me to encourage myself by remembering Your promises for my life. Help me to live my very best life and focus on You.

FOR HEALING

God, You created me for a long and satisfying life. You knit me together in my mother's womb and You know every intricate part of my being. You know what I need before I ask, and I'm asking You to return me to good health. You know how my body and mind work, so You know how to heal me. I refuse to let my health be stolen from me. I am determined to fight for it. Direct me to the right doctors, if that's the way I should go. Give me peace to make the right decisions on my journey to recovery.

TIME AND MOTIVATION FOR FITNESS

Do you not know that your body is a temple of the Holy Spirit,
who is in you, whom you have received from God? You are not your
own; you were bought at a price. Therefore honor God with your body.
1 CORINTHIANS 6:19–20

Lord, I need more time—and motivation—to get in shape. I want to have a fitness routine, but my schedule is crazy; there is always so much to do every day. Show me how to make movement a priority in my life so I will feel better, look better, and have more energy. I want to honor You with my body in my physical health. Lord, I want to be a woman of balance, not extremes. Help me to care for my body and be a wise steward of this resource You've given me all the days of my life.

EATING RIGHT

Go, eat your food with gladness, and drink your wine with
a joyful heart, for it is now that God favors what you do.
ECCLESIASTES 9:7

Lord, I thank You for filling the earth with a bounty of food. I praise You for the variety of fruits, vegetables, proteins, and carbohydrates you provide for sustaining life. Help me to make a priority of eating a nutritious blend of foods, to drink enough water, and to avoid overindulging in junk. I pray for the time to shop and cook balanced meals. Please help me find food that is healthy and good-tasting, and the will to eat in moderation.

WHEN HEALING DOES NOT COME

*I consider that our present sufferings are not worth comparing
with the glory that will be revealed in us. . . . And we know
that in all things God works for the good of those who love
him, who have been called according to his purpose.*
ROMANS 8:18, 28

Lord, I have prayed and healing hasn't come. It's hard to know
why You do not heal when You clearly have the power to do
so. Please help me not to focus on my present suffering, but to
be transformed in my attitude. May I revel in the glory that
will be revealed in me through this and, ultimately, when I am
with You in heaven. I do not understand, but I choose to praise
You anyway. Give me the peace, comfort, and assurance that all
things, even this, will work for my good and for Your glory.

MY HOME—
THE POWER OF HARMONY AND HOSPITALITY

Once upon a time there was a woman who loved God, worked vigorously, and took care of the needs of her family. She also reached out to the poor in her community. This woman was wise and made use of those teachable moments with her kids. And she did it all with strength, dignity, and a smile.

We don't know the woman's name, but we can read about her in Proverbs 31. While our twenty-first-century lives may be vastly different from this industrious woman's experience, certain essentials span the years. The core values of wisdom, faithfulness, dignity, strength, laughter, hard work, helping others, and putting God first still hold as true today as they did some three thousand years ago. The Proverbs 31 woman was an excellent home manager, rewarded with praise from her husband, her kids, and others.

When we are wise stewards of the resources God has provided, our homes can become places of blessing to all who enter. You create the "environment." Will it be a place of warmth and welcome—or an atmosphere of chaos and conflict?

Powerful things happen when you invite *God* to your house. When you call on this gracious guest, He comes every time—and when He does, your home and family will never be the same. "If you are willing to invite God to involve himself in your daily challenges," says Bill Hybels, pastor of Willow Creek Church, "you will experience his prevailing power—in your home, in your relationships, in the marketplace, in schools, in the church, wherever it is most needed. . . . God's prevailing power is released in the lives of people who pray."

Prayer is foundational to every home—whether that's a mansion or a trailer, a cabin or a condo. You can pray power prayers throughout the day, in whatever part of your home you happen to be. Intercede for your husband while you're putting away laundry. Lift up your son's hard day at school while you make dinner. Thank God for the home you have and ask Him to help you wisely manage the resources He has provided.

Pray for protection and safety. Pray for more loving family relationships. Pray for more peace and harmony. Ask God to help your family stay better connected with Him and with one another—in spite of the busyness you all experience. Pray for a heart of hospitality to reach out to friends, neighbors, and your community as a whole.

A home that is built on love and fortified with prayer will stand strong and last long.

A PLACE OF LOVE AND RESPECT

Show proper respect to everyone: Love the brotherhood
of believers, fear God, honor the king.
1 PETER 2:17

Lord, may our home be a place where we show love and respect
to one another. Help us to value each member of our family and
everyone we welcome into our home. We may not always agree;
we may have different opinions. But I pray that we would extend
kindness to others and seek to view them as significant, worthy,
and valuable. We choose to honor others in our home because we
honor You.

HOSPITALITY

Share with God's people who are in need. Practice hospitality.
ROMANS 12:13

Lord, I thank You for my home. Show my heart opportunities to
open this home to others. I want to share what You've provided
for me. As I practice hospitality, may Your love shine through
my life. However my home compares with others', I thank You
for what I have. I am grateful that Your Spirit is present here.
Give me a generous, open heart and use my home for Your good
purposes.

A PLACE TO GROW UP

. . .to prepare God's people for works of service, so that the body of Christ
may be built up until we all reach unity in the faith and in the knowledge
of the Son of God and become mature, attaining to the whole measure of
the fullness of Christ. Then we will no longer be infants, tossed back and
forth by the waves, and blown here and there by every wind of teaching
and by the cunning and craftiness of men in their deceitful scheming.
EPHESIANS 4:12–14

Lord, I ask that our home would be a place where we can mature
in every area of life. Just as we grow up physically, help us to
grow up emotionally and spiritually, too. We don't want to be
childlike and immature, tossed back and forth by the waves of
life's storms or the deceitful ideas of people who seek to mislead
us. Strengthen us in the knowledge of Your ways and help us to
experience Your love and wisdom.

A SAFE PLACE

My people will live in peaceful dwelling places,
in secure homes, in undisturbed places of rest.
ISAIAH 32:18

Lord, I ask that You would be our strong defense and protect our home. May this be a place of safety, comfort, and peace. Guard us from outside forces and protect us from harmful attacks from within. I pray that the Holy Spirit would put a hedge of protection around our home and family. Lord, we look to You as our refuge, our strength, and our security.

ENCOURAGING WORDS

Pleasant words are a honeycomb,
sweet to the soul and healing to the bones.
PROVERBS 16:24

Lord, I pray that we would speak encouraging and kind words in our home. Help us to build one another up—never to tear one another down. Help us not to be so self-absorbed that we forget to ask how others around us are doing. Like honey, may the words from our mouths be sweet to the soul and healing to the bones. Help us to be positive, peaceable, and considerate. Thank You for giving us words that restore.

A FAMILY THAT PRAYS TOGETHER

*He and all his family were devout and God-fearing; he gave
generously to those in need and prayed to God regularly.*
ACTS 10:2

Lord, I want our family to pray together more often. We need
to put You first because You are the source of life—and You are
worthy of our firstfruits of time and attention. Help us make
spending time with You a priority. I pray that meeting with You
together will draw us closer to You and to one another. I believe
You have so much more for us. I ask for Your blessing as we seek
to honor You in this way.

WISE STEWARDSHIP

*The LORD is my strength and my shield;
my heart trusts in him, and I am helped. My heart
leaps for joy and I will give thanks to him in song.*
PSALM 28:7

Lord, I thank You for the household You have entrusted to my
care. Help me to be a wise steward of my resources, of all that
You have provided. Help us to take care of our things, to keep
them clean and in good repair. May we use our money wisely,
may we share freely of Your blessings, and may we spend our
time toward positive ends that bring glory to Your name.

MANAGING YOUR HOUSEHOLD

She watches over the affairs of her household
and does not eat the bread of idleness.
PROVERBS 31:27

Lord, I thank You for the wisdom you give me each day to watch over the affairs of my household. Give me energy to accomplish my work and to keep our home organized and running smoothly. Help me to be a good time manager and to stay centered on Your purposes. I need to get my tasks done, but I also want to nurture and cherish my relationships. Empower me, Lord. Help our home to be a place of order, peace, and enjoyment.

BLESSING FOR A NEW HOUSE

The LORD's curse is on the house of the wicked,
but he blesses the home of the righteous.
PROVERBS 3:33

Lord, please bless this new house. We dedicate it to you in the name of Jesus. We ask that You would bring protection and safety to this place. Fill each room with Your loving presence, Your peace, and Your power. May we treat one another with respect, with warmth and welcome for others. Use this house to bring glory to Your name, Lord. May all who come here feel at home.

MY IDENTITY—THE POWER OF WHO I AM IN CHRIST

One recent graduate, who had not yet decided if she was ready to hit the job market, prepared for the onslaught of questions for back-to-school night at her daughter's elementary school. She had cleverly ordered business cards that read: JULIE STOUT, DOMESTIC ENGINEER, with her home phone and address, cell phone, and e-mail address.

The way we think of ourselves has everything to do with how the world sees us. When you meet someone, the first question you're asked after your name is, "What do you do?" We define one another by what we *do* rather than who we *are*. Often our occupations instead of our commitment to Christ define us to others.

Jesus asked His disciples, "Who do people say I am?" The disciples replied from various people's perspectives, "John the Baptist; others say, Elijah; and still others, one of the prophets." Then Jesus pointed the question at them: "Who do you say I am?" Peter answered, "You are the Christ" (Mark 8:27–29).

Peter recognized Jesus because the Holy Spirit revealed who He was. Through the Holy Spirit's revelation, the disciples saw God when they saw Jesus. He said and did what the Father told Him to do and say. He lived in the power of His heavenly Father's will, consistent with His Father's character.

At some point in your life you were probably introduced to someone based on your relationship with someone else—Annie's sister, Professor Vance's student, or Rich's friend. Now, imagine if you were introduced to others based on your relationship with God. *This is God's child, Stephen. He's the spitting image of his heavenly Father—so strong and courageous.* Or, *C'mon over and meet*

Shelley. She's so compassionate, just like Christ!

As a Christian, your relationship with God should be the foundation of your identity. The only way to find out who you are and who you are meant to be is to discover God's identity and the character that goes along with it.

Ephesians 5:1 says, "Be imitators of God, therefore, as dearly loved children."

Throughout the Bible you read of who God is and how He relates to you. You can find your own identity within the pages that describe His character, His morals, His values, His work ethic—His identity. As you spend time in prayer with Him, you will experience His presence and a personal relationship with Him, and you will grow in His likeness.

The amazing power of who you are in Christ provides you with everything you need to succeed. When you are weak, He is strong. He has made you more than a conqueror, an overcomer in this life. No matter what battles you face, you can do all things through Christ who gives you strength.

A MATTER OF SIGNIFICANCE

Jesus, help me to find my identity in You. I know that my relationship with You is significant. As I read the Bible, give me an understanding of who You created me to be. Point out the true identity that has been given to me through the gift of salvation and my relationship with You.

To them God willed to make known what are the
riches of the glory of this mystery among the Gentiles:
which is Christ in you, the hope of glory.
COLOSSIANS 1:27 NKJV

FACING THE TRUTH

Lord, I know I need to change a lot of things in my life. Thank You for accepting me as I am, where I am today. You see the potential of who I can be, even when I can't see it. Show me the things in my heart that You want to change. Open my eyes; I don't want to pretend anymore. Help me see the truth so You can make me new!

A VOTE OF CONFIDENCE

I don't want to pretend to be someone I'm not. Help me to stand up to the pressure that others place on me to conform. Lord, You are my confidence! I can do all things through Jesus Christ who gives me strength to face today's challenges—even when those challenges are people. Give me the words to stay true to my commitment to You. I remind myself of all the things that You have done, all the battles You have fought on my behalf. With You at my side and in my heart, I know I can succeed.

AN IMITATOR OF GOD

Father, my relationship with You affects my personality in amazing ways. Many people have a negative idea of what it means to be a Christian. Forgive me when I've failed to be like You. I want to be so full of Your presence that others see You in everything I say and do. I never want anything I do to reflect negatively on You. I want to be like Jesus, of whom people said, "Truly this was the Son of God!" (Matthew 27:54 NKJV).

FINDING COURAGE

Jesus, thank You for the courage to live my life following Your example. I can do all things through You who gives me the power to succeed. I refuse to be intimidated by what others say, think, or do. I live my life according to our Father's will and the Holy Spirit's instruction. Help me to declare to others the freedom I have found in You, so I point the way to You. Equip me to lead others to follow You.

FINDING ASSURANCE

When people see me, let them see You. Help me not to confuse who You say I am with self-confidence, arrogance, or pride. My confidence is only because You live in and through me. Give me wisdom to know when to speak and when to listen so others may know You through my actions.

LIVING WITHOUT GUILT OR SHAME

I have a list of things that make me feel guilty. They shout at me. I've told You my sins, and You have forgiven me, but I remember. Lord, help me to let go of my past mistakes. Help me to forgive myself. These things are like heavy chains keeping me from living the life of freedom that comes from a relationship with You. Today, I lift them off my shoulders and leave them at Your feet. Help me to never pick them up again. I let them go now. I am free today in Jesus' name!

LIFE FROM A POSITIVE PERSPECTIVE

As I learn who I am in Christ, I realize that I need to look at life from a positive perspective. My life in You is not about what I'm missing or don't have. It's about Your light and life working in and through me. In even the most difficult situations I will find Your goodness in me.

NOTHING MISSING—COMPLETE

I always felt I was missing something in my life before I met You. You are the missing piece of the puzzle. Now, no matter what I face, I know that I lack no good thing. When I am weak, You are strong. Instead of discouragement, I have boldness to do the things that without You I couldn't do. When life is a mess, You comfort me with Your peace. With You in my life, I am complete. All I need is You—nothing else.

TO LIVE IN CHRIST

In Your love and mercy You gave me life when You raised Christ from the dead. I was lost and alone, but You found me. You picked me up and gave me all the benefits of Your own Son, Jesus. Thank You for Your incredible kindness. All I had to do was believe and receive this gift. I can't take credit for it—it was all You! Father, continue to make me new each day in Christ.

TO BE A PEACEMAKER

Jesus, You said, "Blessed are the peacemakers, for they will be called sons of God" (Matthew 5:9). I want to be a peacemaker because it brings me closer to You. Help me to be open to other points of view and to think before I talk. Show me Your plan of peace in difficult situations. Remind me that it's more important to let others see You in me than to prove to them that I am right. When there doesn't seem to be a peaceful solution, show me Your way to peace.

LET LOVE RULE

Lord, help me to get rid of anger, cruelty, slander, and dirty language. I have the mind of Christ and can exercise self-control. Show me how to live my life with mercy, kindness, humility, gentleness, and patience. Remind me to allow for others' faults, even when they don't allow for mine. I want to be quick to forgive. Above all, help me to let Christ govern my heart. Please forgive me when I forget and take control.

IN THE FACE OF PREJUDICE

All men and women are equal in Your sight. Jesus died for every one of us, no matter where we come from or what color our skin is. Help me not to value one relationship over another because of influence, wealth, intellect, or race. Help me to see others from Your perspective, no matter how different other people are from me. Help me to love them and learn from the differences we have.

PURE MOTIVES

Lord, help me to examine my motives in pursuit of friendship. Why do I seek relationships with certain people? Give me the courage to look truthfully into my heart and see my true intentions. Sometimes I think a relationship with a certain person might help me look better in the eyes of others. I am ambitious, but I know it's wrong to use people to get what I want. You supply everything I need. Help me to maintain right and pure relationships before You.

MY INNER LIFE—
THE POWER OF CHRIST-CENTERED LIVING

We want to make prayer a priority, but we're chasing wandering toddlers all day. Or we'd love to sit on the sofa, reflecting on the goodness of God—but we have to get up at 5:00 a.m. for a long commute to work. The hectic pace of daily life often makes us feel more like human *doings* than human *beings*. Prayer, reflection, and rest become the empty rooms in our house of self when we don't make time for them. We need the power of the Holy Spirit to get our interior lives redecorated.

Cultivating our inner lives is not selfish—it's smart and it's biblical. God values the inner life; the beauty of a gentle and quiet spirit is of great worth to Him (1 Peter 3:4). In Proverbs 4:23 we are admonished to guard our hearts, the wellspring of life.

Taking care of ourselves, both inside and out, is vital to our survival. When our identity is solidly rooted in who we are in Christ, we have more confidence. Reconnected to the Source of power and love—God Almighty—we have the resources to be cleansed, healed, and filled. And when we are rested and replenished, we have more to give away to others.

Though God isn't finished with any of us yet, we can still have powerful prayer lives when we are well fed spiritually. Ask God for a hunger for His Word. Take time to think about what you read, and meditate on it. Pray that God would reveal to you your true worth and value in His eyes. Ask Him to help you become a woman of character and integrity, to mean what you say and to keep your promises and commitments. Pray against temptation and for the power to flee it. Don't let the evil one mess with you—ask God for help (Matthew 26:41).

Pray for the Lord to strengthen your life from the inside out. Pray to be more positive and friendly and to speak with truth and kindness. If you ask, He will help you find a way. He loves a gentle and quiet spirit!

CLEANSE MY HEART

Lord, I humbly ask for forgiveness of sin in my life. I repent and turn from doing those wrong things. I don't know why I do the things I don't want to do. Sometimes it's willful and sometimes I'm just careless. Thank You for Your loving-kindness and mercy that cleanse my soul and let me be in right standing with You again. Cleanse me, heal me, and make me whole, Lord.

EMPOWER MY LIFE

Holy Spirit, I cannot live life in my own strength. I ask that You would come and fill me with Your presence. Empower me with discernment to make better life choices and energy to thrive—not just survive. Give me a heart to seek You and serve others. Pour into my life more love, joy, peace, and patience—to be a caring mom, a loving wife, a good friend, a wise worker—a woman who is blessed, Lord.

MAKING PRAYER A PRIORITY

*"But blessed is the man who trusts in the LORD,
whose confidence is in him."*
JEREMIAH 17:7

Lord, I feel like a withered plant with dry, brown leaves. Help me connect with You in prayer so I can grow strong and healthy, inside and out, like a vibrant green tree. You are my source of living water. Teach me to be still, to listen, to absorb what You want to reveal to me in this time of inward filling. In this holy conversation, may I find freedom, peace, and joy—and a closer walk with You.

LIVING A LIFE OF LOVE

"Love your neighbor as yourself."
MATTHEW 22:39

Lord, I want to live a life of love! Show me what true love is—Your love—so I can receive it and give it away to others. Teach me to care for my neighbor as I would care for myself. Let love be my motivation for action. Help me to speak kind, encouraging words and to bless others with my actions as well. I thank You that Your amazing, unconditional, accepting love sustains me.

KNOWING YOUR WORTH AND VALUE

Lord, I have sought to find my significance places other than Your heart. Forgive me for putting weight in what other people think, or in my own efforts. I thank You that You value me because I am Your child—and that I have great worth no matter what I look like or do for a living. You find the unfading beauty of a gentle and quiet spirit to be of great worth in Your sight. Thank You for loving and valuing me, Lord.

BEAUTIFUL INSIDE AND OUT

Lord, our world is so focused on outward appearance—nice clothes and good looks. But You're never like that. People may look at the hairstyles and the outfits, but You look at the heart. Lord, please help me to work with what You've given me on the outside—as I also polish my inner character. May Your beauty shine through me as I praise You more and more. Be my Light within that I may radiate the love of Christ.

A PERSON OF WISDOM

*Blessed is the man who finds wisdom, the man
who gains understanding, for she is more profitable
than silver and yields better returns than gold.*
PROVERBS 3:13–14

Lord, I want to be a person of wisdom, not foolishness. Help me
to make right choices and conduct myself in a manner worthy
of Your name. I pray that I would be honest and upright in
my daily life so my actions reflect who You are. Help me to act
with integrity so I become a person who keeps promises and
commitments.

CONFIDENCE

*The LORD will be your confidence and
will keep your foot from being snared.*
PROVERBS 3:26

Lord, help me to have more confidence—not in myself but in
You. I don't want to be proud or conceited, but I don't want to
be a doormat, either. Give me a teachable heart. You have so
much to show me, and I want to learn Your ways. Learning and
growing, I am alive! I am totally dependent on You, Lord. Full of
Your Spirit, I can stand confident and strong.

SELF-CONTROL

Lord, I need Your help. Please create in me the fruit of self-control—in all areas of my life. Empower me to walk in Your Spirit's power and to flee temptation. Help me to change the channel or walk away from the food or put my credit cards out of reach when I've been using them too much. Give me the strength I need to stay pure—both sexually and emotionally—around men to whom I am not married. Keep me, Lord, in the center of Your will.

ACCOUNTABILITY

Lord, I pray for someone with whom I can share my inner life—someone who will hold me accountable. Please provide a mature woman who will mentor me and keep my life struggles confidential. I pray for someone with a loving heart—a person who won't judge me, but who will pray for and with me. Help me to be wise and responsible, but when I'm not, Lord, help me learn and grow in my spiritual development. I want to be strong in Your strength.

THE VALUE OF REST

Lord, I come to You for respite. Like a rest in music breaks the tension, I need a break, too. Whether it's a quarter rest, like a nap, or a whole rest, like a good night's sleep or a day off, may I find healing and strength in quietness and solitude. Give me the courage to be still, to cease striving, and to be with You. Replenish me in Your presence, Lord.

Do you not know? Have you not heard? The Lord is the everlasting God, the Creator of the ends of the earth. He will not grow tired or weary, and his understanding no one can fathom.
ISAIAH 40:28

DEVELOPING CREATIVITY

Lord, I thank You for the gift of creativity. I praise You for the ability to use my hands to work at a skill and my mind to process ideas. As I photograph a sunset, or till my garden, or start a new quilt, or spend time in nature, I praise You, my Creator. No one can fathom Your greatness and Your limitless creative ideas. The whole world is Your canvas and the earth's beauty a work of art. Help me to grow in developing my creative abilities.

ATTITUDE

Lord, I pray for a good attitude today. Help me to be a woman who is positive and joyful, not sarcastic or cutting. May I learn to have the mind of Christ, with an outlook that seeks to build others up, not tear them down. I pray that I would not be self-centered but aware of the needs of others, seeking to meet them with God's help. Help me to see others from Your loving point of view.

DEALING WITH PRIDE

For by the grace given me I say to every one of you:
Do not think of yourself more highly than you ought,
but rather think of yourself with sober judgment,
in accordance with the measure of faith God has given you.
ROMANS 12:3

Lord, Your Word says that we are not to think of ourselves more highly than we ought, but to think of ourselves with sober judgment, in accordance with the faith You have given us. Help me not to have pride, arrogance, or conceit in my heart—but when I do, please forgive me. Humble me, Lord, and lift me up to be a willing servant. With my eyes on You, not on myself, may I see the needs in the lives of others.

YOU DON'T HAVE TO BE PERFECT

For the law was given through Moses;
grace and truth came through Jesus Christ.
JOHN 1:17

Lord, when I struggle with perfectionism, help me to break this bondage in my life. I know it's a good thing to want things to be right, but it's possible to go too far. I want to live in Your grace, not under the "law" that keeps me under this burden. Heal me, Lord, from judging myself and my actions too harshly—and fearing the judgment of others. Help me to see, Lord, that because of Your mercy and grace, I am good enough.

A THANKFUL HEART

Be joyful always; pray continually; give thanks in
all circumstances, for this is God's will for you in Christ Jesus.
1 THESSALONIANS 5:16–18

Lord, You are my God—and it is my joy to give You my inner heart. Cleanse me, fill me, heal me, and help me to live with a joyful, thankful heart. I want to be a woman of prayer. I want to make a difference in my world. For all You are and all You do, I am grateful. I give You praise for the blessings in my life.

MY JOY—THE POWER OF OBEDIENCE

Where does joy come from? From winning a trip to Hawaii? Is it in the bliss of a newborn baby? Or maybe from the calm delight of watching a sunset with the one you love? Those things may bring us happiness, but what happens when it rains at the beach, the baby has colic, or the one you love no longer wants to watch sunsets with you?

True joy is not fleeting, nor dependent on our circumstances. Though the world may seem intent on squelching our happiness, we can learn to pray powerfully for more *joy* in our lives. It starts with asking.

"This is the confidence we have in approaching God," the apostle John wrote in 1 John 5:14–15, "that if we ask anything according to his will, he hears us. And if we know that he hears us—whatever we ask—we know that we have what we asked of him."

Of course, the timing is God's prerogative. A woman named Sarah knew that God answers prayer, but she wasn't willing to wait on Him. She wanted a son, and in spite of God's promise to her husband, Abraham, she tried to arrange for the baby's birth by a surrogate, her servant Hagar. Hagar's son, Ishmael, caused much grief to Sarah—but God was gracious and ultimately provided Sarah the son, Isaac, He had promised long before. "God has brought me laughter, and everyone who hears about this will laugh with me," Sarah said finally (Genesis 21:6).

In surrendering our will for God's will and following His commands, we can realize more of God's power and joy in our lives. Jesus said, "If you obey my commands, you will remain in my love, just as I have obeyed my Father's commands and remain in his love. I have told you this so that my joy may be in you and that your joy may be complete" (John 15:10–11).

A heart full of joy is a heart that sings praise and thanks to God. Praising Him multiplies our joy and increases our faith. "Praise is the spark plug of faith," says Kay Arthur in *When Bad Things Happen.* "Praise gets faith airborne, where it can soar above the gravitational forces of this world's cares. The secret of faith is continual praise even when your inward parts tremble, lips quiver, and decay enters your bones."

Praising and thanking God—for who He is and all He has done—will make any hard day better. "The LORD is my strength and my shield," the psalmist wrote. "My heart trusts in him, and I am helped. My heart leaps for joy and I will give thanks to him in song" (Psalm 28:7).

FINDING STRENGTH

Lord, I am tired and weary. Infuse me with life, energy, and joy again. I thank You for being my strength and my joy. I don't have to look to a bowl of ice cream or the compliments of a friend to fill me up on the inside. Steady and constant, You are my Source; You are the One who fills me. Sustain me, Lord, with the power of Your love, so I can live my life refreshed and renewed.

JOY DESPITE TRIALS

Lord, it seems odd to consider trials a joyful thing. But I pray that my challenges in life, these times of testing, will lead me to greater perseverance. May that perseverance finish its work so I will be mature and complete, on my way to wholeness. I ask for wisdom and Your perspective as I seek joy in the hard times— and the better times that will come my way.

THE JOY OF KNOWING JESUS

Jesus, knowing You brings me joy! I am so glad that I am saved and on my way to heaven. Thank You for the abundant life You provide. I can smile because I know that You love me. I can be positive because You have the power to heal, restore, and revive. Your presence brings me joy—just being with You is such a privilege. You are awesome, and I delight to know You and tell others about You.

But let all who take refuge in you be glad;
let them ever sing for joy. Spread your protection over them,
that those who love your name may rejoice in you.
PSALM 5:11

JOY IN GOD'S PROTECTION

Lord, please cover me. Protect me from my enemies—fear and doubt, worry and human reasoning. I try to figure everything out, but I end up confused and tired. Let me rest in the comfort of Your love and the safety of Your protection. Here, abiding in You, I am secure and I am glad. Spread your consolation over me as I rejoice in You. You are my joy and my protection, Lord.

REAL AND LASTING JOY

Lord, I am so tired of imitations. People pretend to be something they're not. Food is flavored with artificial ingredients. It's hard to tell what is false and what is true anymore. When it comes to joy, I want the real thing. Pour into my life Your genuine and lasting joy. I need more of You, Lord. I pray for righteousness, peace, and joy in the Holy Spirit. Fill me, please.

JOY IN PRAYING FOR OTHERS

Lord, I thank You for the joy and privilege of praying for others. What a blessing to be able to intercede, to stand in the gap and move heaven and earth for those I love. In all my prayers for those I know, may I have a heart of joy. Bless my family and friends, Lord. Bless those who need You today. May I find pleasure and delight in lifting up prayers for others.

FINDING JOY IN GOD'S PRESENCE

Lord, draw me closer to You. In Your presence is fullness of joy—and I want to be filled. Knowing I am loved by You makes me glad; I cannot imagine life without You. With You there is light; without You, darkness. With You there is pleasure; without You, pain. You care, You comfort; You really listen. Here, in Your presence, I am loved, I am renewed, and I am very happy.

> *The LORD has done great things for us,*
> *and we are filled with joy.*
> PSALM 126:3

OBEDIENCE LEADS TO JOY

"As the Father has loved me, so have I loved you. Now remain in my love. If you obey my commands, you will remain in my love, just as I have obeyed my Father's commands and remain in his love. I have told you this so that my joy may be in you and that your joy may be complete."
JOHN 15:9–11

Lord, Your Word says that if we obey Your commands, we will remain in Your love. I want to serve You out of an obedient, not a rebellious, heart. Just as Jesus submits to You, Father, I choose to submit to You, too. Obedience leads to a blessing. Empower me, encourage me, and give me the will to want to make right decisions, decisions that lead to a better life and greater joy.

LIVING DAILY WITH DELIGHT

*"You will go out in joy and be led forth in peace;
the mountains and hills will burst into song before you,
and all the trees of the field will clap their hands."*
ISAIAH 55:12

Lord, I thank You for the joy You bring every day. Whether I go out or stay in, joy is with me—because You are there. Lead me forth today in peace. May all of creation—even the trees of the field—praise You as I praise You. Help me to live with a lighter heart and a positive attitude, despite the distractions and duties that seek to steal my joy. I choose You. Help me to live daily with Your delight.

ENJOYING GOD'S BLESSINGS

Lord, I thank You for the work of Your hands. A wildflower, a mountain scene, the ocean waves on a white sand beach—the beauty of the earth reveals Your glory. Thank You for the smile of a child, the touch of my beloved's hand, the warmth of our home. I am grateful for the love of friends and meaningful work. You have done great things for us, and we are filled with joy. Thank You for Your many blessings.

TURNING SORROW TO JOY

Lord, I give You my sorrow and I ask for joy. I give You my pain and I ask for healing. I give You my fears and I ask for freedom and peace. Deliver me. Giver of good gifts, may I find a heart of gladness. In Your mercy and love, let me be a woman of courage, conviction, and confidence. Side by side, may I be in step with the Spirit as we journey through life together.

JOY OF PRAISE

Lord, I lift up my hands to You and praise You! You are worthy of worship. From You all blessings come. You are the One who heals. You bring mercy and justice. Thank You for Your goodness and grace. I praise You for Your kindness and consolation. Faithful One, I adore You; I honor You. My lips shout for joy when I sing praises to You, my Lord and my Redeemer.

JOYFUL VIEWPOINT

Father, as evening approached, the landscape had become bleak and desolate. We'd driven through a valley that was deep in shadow. But we topped the ridge and stopped at a lookout. The setting sun gave us a view of gold-tinged beauty. The point of view made all the difference. When I'm in sorrow, I can see joy, provided I allow You to illuminate my life. Lord, keep me walking in the joy of Your light.

ERASING THE GLOOM

Lord, help me make joy an integral part of my personality. May I be filled with joy even when I'm in distress for physical or emotional reasons. May I avoid dwelling on the negative aspects of my life that I encounter each day. Instead, help me erase the gloom and replace it with the warm comfort of Your love. Let me turn to You, the source of my joy.

I NEED MORE JOY

Lord, buoy my spirits. I need more joy in my life. Daily living and trials can be so depleting; I just can't do it on my own. Help me to laugh more and enjoy life again. Help me to have a childlike, playful spirit—a lighter heart, Lord. Encourage me so I can bless others with a kind word or a smile. Let me come to Your dwelling place and find strength and joy in praising You. In Your presence is fullness of joy!

FEAR AND JOY

Lord, fear is ugly and joy is beautiful. When fear is vanquished, joy becomes even more beautiful. So many people have a beautiful smile as they decide to follow You. They have replaced fear with the knowledge that they are following the One who sets aside all fear. I pray I will extinguish fear by remembering that I can put my trust in You.

MY MARRIAGE—THE POWER OF LOVE

Larry Burkett wrote, "There are times in every marriage when it seems barely tolerable." So after two people have fallen in love and said, "I do," how do they keep from later saying, "I don't anymore"?

First, we need to understand that, from the very beginning, men and women were made for each other: "And the LORD God said, 'It is not good that man should be alone; I will make him a helper'" (Genesis 2:18 NKJV). God has planted a desire within us to have a relationship not only with Him, but with a member of the opposite sex.

Next, we need to acknowledge that, as Richard J. Foster wrote, "God desires that marriages be healthy, whole, and permanent." In spite of our differences in background, personality, likes, and dislikes, we need to become compatible. Larry Burkett wrote, "If two people in a marriage are just alike one of them is unnecessary. In great part, God puts opposites together. . .so that one will offset the extremes of the other one. If we look at differences as a problem rather than as a balance, we will end up arguing a lot. By recognizing the differences as an asset, a couple can become one working unit. That is what God desires."

When you and your spouse said, "I do," you promised to love, honor, and cherish each other "until death do [you] part." That's quite a vow of commitment to make before family, friends, and God. And it is one you are meant to keep. The great thing about marriage is that, as the years go by, it gets better and better, not only in spite of but perhaps because of the bumps along the way. The power of staunch commitment is an awesome thing when combined with the power of love.

Once committed, you need to communicate. Don't become so caught up in the world that you become two ships passing in the night, merely blaring your horns once in a while and then heading into separate seas. And when you do converse, watch your words. Sometimes during a heated argument things are said that you cannot take back. And you need not only to *watch* what you say but to *mean* what you say.

Now that you're communicating, take the time to compliment each other. As the years progress, husbands and wives tend to get into a rut. Prevent your rut from becoming a chasm by "rejoic[ing] in the wife [or husband] of your youth" (Proverbs 5:18). When you work at praising and complimenting each other day after day, the flame of your love will burn ever greater, and you'll find yourselves rejoicing in each other's presence.

But commitment, communication, and compliments will be hollow at best unless you care for each other using the power of the *love* described in 1 Corinthians 13:4–8. Make it a point to practice this love every day.

TWO IN ONE

Lord, my spouse and I are two who have been united into one. I praise You and thank You for leading me to my other half. He is more than I ever could have hoped for or dreamed. Bless our marriage, bless our union, bless our lives. Help us to grow closer together with each passing year. Lead us to do what You have called us to do, as one standing before You this day.

MY REWARD IN LIFE

Life passes so quickly, Lord. Yet for this precious amount of time I have here on earth, I want to enjoy life with my spouse. He is so dear to me. Thank You for rewarding me with his presence in the morning as I wake and at night when the lights go out. Thank You for filling me with thoughts of my lover throughout the day. Bless my spouse this morning. Let Your love flow through me and into my other half.

GETTING STRONGER EVERY DAY

Lord, my spouse and I have been through such trials, yet each time we make it over a hurdle together, our love grows stronger. What we had in the beginning of our marriage was good, but what we have now is better. Continue to help us through the trials of this life. Help us to keep a united front before our children. And in all things, may we praise Your name for the wonders and joy of marital love.

A FRESH PASSION

I feel as if we are just going through the motions, Lord. Could it be that we have fallen out of love with each other? But that's not what marriage is all about, is it? There are times when it feels as if we have fallen out of love, but we still do care deeply for each other. Help us to remain patient. Help our love to bloom anew. Give us a fresh passion for each other. Light the flame of our desire, Lord. Keep us as one.

MAKING LOVE

Thank You, Lord, for the intimacy my spouse and I share. Thank You for the children who have come as a result of our union. They are truly our treasure. Continue to give us the desire for each other, for the times of passion and the times of cuddling. It is like heaven on earth. Bless my spouse this day. Give him the strength to meet the challenges ahead. Bring him home safely and into my loving arms.

CHOOSING WORDS CAREFULLY

I did it again, Lord. I spoke before I thought and now I have wounded my spouse. According to Your Word, there is more hope for a fool than for me. I feel so terrible about what I said. I know I cannot take away the words I have spoken. All I can say is that I'm sorry. Forgive me, Father, for the words I spoke. My heart is so heavy within me. Give me the courage to ask my spouse for forgiveness. And may this rift in our union be speedily mended. Heal our marriage, Lord. Give me hope.

RECORD OF WRONGS

[Love] does not demand its own way.
It is not irritable, and it keeps no record of being wronged.
1 CORINTHIANS 13:5 NLT

I can't seem to help myself, Lord. I have this list in my mind of all the things my spouse has done to hurt me. I cannot seem to let them go. And it is harming our marriage. Help me to give up on this record of wrongs. Give us a clean slate this morning and every morning. Help me not to keep on bringing up the past but to just have hope for tomorrow. May the power of love erase all these wrongs and give us back the magic of yesterday.

UNDYING LOVE

Love never gives up, never loses faith, is always
hopeful, and endures through every circumstance.
1 CORINTHIANS 13:7 NLT

My love for my spouse will never die, Lord, because we believe in You. We know You have brought us together and will keep us together. We will never give up on this marriage, nor lose faith in each other, nor lose hope in our circumstances. We are in this until the end and, although we may not love every minute of it, we do love each other and You. And because of that, we are growing stronger every day. Thank You, Jesus, for the power of love!

LORD, CHANGE ME

Lord, look into my life and search my heart. Is there anything hurtful that I have been doing? Remove the sin and selfishness. Help me to stop focusing on how my spouse should change. Lord, cleanse *my* heart first. I can't change anyone else, so I ask You to show me what needs to go from my life, what needs to stay, and how I can be right with You. As You do, I pray for greater love and healing in our marriage.

LOVE EACH OTHER

Lord, You are the author of love. Teach us to love each other deeply, from the heart. I thank You for the love my spouse and I share, for the joy and the closeness. When we do something wrong, help each of us to forgive and move past the offense. I pray that our love would be patient and kind, not proud or selfish, but seeking each other's good. Protect our love and keep our marriage solid as we put our hope and trust in You.

DEAL WITH ANGER

"In your anger do not sin": Do not let the
sun go down while you are still angry.
Ephesians 4:26

Lord, I need Your help in dealing with my anger, whether I am simply annoyed, a little mad, or downright furious. I want to handle this feeling in healthy ways. Help me to process my emotions and not let them fester inside me. Help me to control my temper and talk about what bothers me in calmer ways. Show me how to give my anger to You so I can live in peace with my spouse.

FORGIVE EACH OTHER

Get rid of all bitterness, rage and anger,
brawling and slander, along with every form of malice.
Ephesians 4:31

Lord, I don't know why forgiveness can sometimes be so hard. We need Your help to get rid of bitterness and anger in our marriage. Help us to build each other up instead of putting each other down—even when it seems we deserve the latter. Teach us grace. Help us to forgive one another and to be kind and compassionate, because we know Christ forgave each of us.

LIVE IN UNITY

Lord, I humbly ask that we would be united and strong as a couple. May Your cords of peace, honor, respect, and love hold us together during both the good times and the challenges of our married life. As we become more connected to You, Lord, help us to be closer to each other. Help us to be patient, bearing with each other in love. And help us to live in joyful harmony.

KEEP US FROM WANDERING

Lord, I ask in the name and power of Jesus that You would keep my husband and me from straying from our marriage vows. Keep our eyes from wandering and our hearts pure—toward you and toward each other—so that we never give in to an emotional or sexual intimacy outside our marriage. Help us not to discredit our union but rather to stay faithful—and to cherish the special connecting bond we have with each other.

FUN AND FRIENDSHIP

Lord, I thank You for the bond of friendship in our marriage. I enjoy talking and sharing life with my husband. Thank You for our laughter and joy. Help us to keep our attitude positive, to smile and have fun together. Give us time to reconnect on a playful level—in sports, games, travel, or working together around the house. Keep us connected in love and friendship and help us to truly enjoy each other.

Two are better than one, because they have a good return
for their work: If one falls down, his friend can help him up.
But pity the man who falls and has no one to help him up!
ECCLESIASTES 4:9–10

THANK YOU FOR OUR MARRIAGE

Lord, I thank You for my husband and for our marriage. We can lift each other up, encourage each other, and go through life together with true companionship. We are a team and You are our Captain. I ask that You would continue to enrich this relationship so we can grow together, in both good times and bad. As we learn to love You more, and our love for each other grows, help us to reach out and be a blessing to others.

MY MINISTRY—THE POWER OF BEING REAL

Reality television seems to catch people in the act of everyday life, showing all the world the truth about those involved in normal—and not so normal—situations. What if you lived your life similar to a reality show, where the world could look in and see the real you, transparent at all times?

Do you ever find yourself pretending to be someone you're not? How many times have you hidden your emotions and told someone you were okay when your feelings were hurt or you were angry? Maybe there were times when you told people what you thought they wanted to hear instead of being truthful with them.

In the book *Unchristian* by David Kinnaman and Gabe Lyons, a major research project conducted by the Barna Group explains that Christianity has an image problem. The study provides detailed insight into the opinions of sixteen- to twenty-nine-year-olds, demonstrating that Christians have almost completely failed in one of their most important assignments—representing Christ to the world.

Today Christians are perceived as being no different than those outside the church. Christians deal with the same problems as unbelievers. The divorce rate; indebtedness; and mental, emotional, and physical-appearance issues are no different. Looking from the outside in, it doesn't appear that Christians have anything to give the world.

People are looking for answers. They are disappointed to find that even those who believe in a loving God are indifferent toward pointing others to Him with the same mission and vision that Jesus demonstrated. Jesus was unconventional. He opposed the religious, man-made interpretations of the law and looked to the heart of those who were outcasts, sick, and hurting. He cared about the ones society ignored.

God wants us to set ourselves apart for His service. We are called to be examples to those who do not know Him. We have to get outside the four walls of the church and live in a way that demonstrates to others what God is like. Like Jesus, we must say and do only what the Father tells us to say and do. We must be real—true to the Word of God, following Jesus, and modeling His example. He demonstrated love for the lost, those society had thrown away. He came to testify to the truth that God loves each one of us.

As you go about your daily life, ask God to show you the power of living a transparent life. Let Him help you shake off the facade of what you believe others would want you to be and step into the light of God's truth.

GENUINE AUTHENTICITY

Lord, help me to be a true reflection of Your heart in all that I do. Help me to take off the mask when I'm tempted to hide my true self. Remind me that my actions should not be for attention, praise, or position. I want my motives to always be pure. Help me to discern my real intentions when I decide to do something. Keep me honest and remind me that I represent You in the choices I make. In everything I pursue, help me above all to be committed to my relationship with You.

> *"These people show honor to me with words,*
> *but their hearts are far from me."*
> MATTHEW 15:8 NCV

REAL RELATIONSHIP

God, I want to be real in my relationships. I want others to see You working in my life. Help me to shift my focus from myself to those around me. I don't want my life to be consumed by empty religion and man-made rules. May my words be a reflection of a heart that is full of Your love and Your life.

LIVING SACRIFICES

*Therefore, I urge you, brothers, in view of God's mercy,
to offer your bodies as living sacrifices, holy and pleasing
to God—this is your spiritual act of worship.*
ROMANS 12:1

Here I am, Lord, lifting myself up to You this morning. I want to serve You. I live to please You, for I love You with all my strength, soul, mind, heart, and body. I dedicate myself, my time, and my service to You. Show me the path You want me to take so that at the end of my days, when I see Your smiling face, You will say, "She did what she could."

FINDING YOUR GIFT

*Don't act thoughtlessly, but understand
what the Lord wants you to do.*
EPHESIANS 5:17 NLT

Lord, I'm looking for direction. I'm not sure how You want me to serve You. So many times I feel so inadequate, that others can do things better than I ever could. But I know those feelings are not of You. Help me to understand, Lord, how You want me to serve, what You want me to do. Not worrying about pleasing others but pleasing You, I will do so all to Your glory.

SERVING FROM THE HEART

As slaves of Christ, do the will of God with all your heart.
EPHESIANS 6:6 NLT

I want to work for You, Lord, using all my heart, soul, and talent.
I want to be Your tool, serving You with passion. And as I do
so, help me to keep my eyes and focus on You, and not on the
gift You have given me. Help me to understand what You have
shaped me to do.

CREATED FOR GOOD WORKS

We are God's masterpiece. He has created us anew in Christ Jesus,
so we can do the good things he planned for us long ago.
EPHESIANS 2:10 NLT

You have shaped me into the unique person I am today. You
have created me to do good works. I am awed that You prepared
things in advance for me to do. From the very beginning, You
made me for a specific job in Your kingdom. Give me the
courage to take hold of that task. Help me not to shy away from
the challenges that face me.

WHEN OTHERS OPPOSE ME

Jesus, sometimes I am tempted to believe I am more spiritual and deserving than others. I know You don't condone that attitude. It makes me angry when others make fun of what I believe, and I am ready to defend my beliefs. Help me to consider their feelings and the possibility that they don't understand where I'm coming from. Remind me that being right is less important than being Your servant. Help me to be a positive influence on those You bring into my life.

LEGITIMATE FAITH

Lord, I don't want to fake it! I'm tired of saying one thing and doing another. Forgive me for pretending to have it all together. I don't want to be a wishy-washy Christian. Help me to trust You and believe the promises You have given me in Your Word. I believe—help my unbelief.

TO LIVE WHAT I BELIEVE

Lord, forgive me when my choices don't line up with what I say I believe. Help me to nurture Your Word in my heart so I grow to maturity. Teach me Your ways and give me understanding of Your instructions. Allow the values of my faith to affect every area of my life. Convict me of sin when I am tempted to stray from truth. Help me to stay committed to living what I believe as I grow in faith and in my relationship with You.

> *Walk by the Spirit, and you will not*
> *carry out the desire of the flesh.*
> GALATIANS 5:16 NASB

TO STAY CONNECTED

God, there are so many distractions—so many things I feel I have to do. Help me to stay connected to You throughout my day. I want to share it with You and be used by You to reach others. Speak to my heart and remind me that You have something for me to do today. Lead me by Your Spirit.

FILL ME WITH LOVE

God, You are love. Everything You do is because of love, and the motive behind those actions is love. I want to be a catalyst of love in the lives of others, too. Forgive me when I think first of myself. Help me to prefer others. Help my love for others to grow. Give me compassion and opportunities to demonstrate it. Lord, it's not about me; it's about You and those You want to touch through me. Help me learn to let Your love flow through me to others.

FOR BOLDNESS IN MINISTRY

Lord, I don't know where to start in sharing my faith with others. When You give me the opportunity, help me to realize You are opening the door. Help me to recognize Your timing and to follow Your leading. Speak to me and through me. Give me Your words that will touch others' hearts and turn them toward a relationship with You.

SHARING MY CHALLENGES

Father, You know all I have gone through in my life, all of my hurts and pains. I know I went through those difficulties for a reason, perhaps to encourage others. Help me to be quick to share with anyone who might benefit from what I have endured. Help me to share how I learned to trust in You as You brought me through each challenge. Strengthen those people with boldness and courage. Give me the words to encourage them to hold tightly to You during their hardships.

Be an example to the believers with your words,
your actions, your love, your faith, and your pure life.
1 TIMOTHY 4:12 NCV

WHEN OTHERS ARE WATCHING

It's hard to be an example, Lord. I don't do everything the way I know I should. I want to be strong and diligent to do what is right. Help me hold fast to my convictions. Help me to be honest when I make mistakes. I want to encourage others by following You faithfully. Give me courage and strength to live my life to please You so I can say to them, "Follow me, as I follow Christ."

FINDING THE REAL ME

Lord, I want to be everything You created me to be. Give me courage to express myself no matter who is around. Help me not to fear what other people think or say about me, but help me to trust You to protect me from potential hurt. Help me to find the real me—the unique person You created me to be. And show me how to express myself in ways that honor You.

INSIDE AND OUT

God, I want to live from the inside out. I want people to experience the real me every time we meet. Help me to examine the values that direct my life. Help me to know what I believe and why I believe it. You know the things I struggle with. Give me Your grace and strength as I learn and grow in those areas. I want to honor You in everything I do.

MY PASSION—THE POWER OF THE HEART

Undoubtedly you've felt your heart tremble at all that's going on in your life. So many emotions: excitement, enthusiasm, uncertainty, pride. What is the fuel that fires the passion in your heart?

The word *passion* can describe romantic feelings; a drive to excel in sports, business, or a dream; or how someone feels about material items they collect. In the context of Jesus' life, passion means to suffer. It is to want something so badly that you're willing to sacrifice anything to have it. God's desire to have a relationship with you was so great that He sacrificed His only Son to have the opportunity to be a part of your life for all eternity.

Augustine is accepted by most scholars as the most important figure in the ancient Western church. His prayer, "For You have created us for Yourself, O Lord, and our hearts are restless until they rest in Thee," demonstrates the passionate cry of the human heart for something bigger than itself.

Unfortunately, people worldwide spend their lives searching for fulfillment from something or someone other than God. In their search, they substitute God's place in their hearts with false passions such as careers, sports, and relationships.

Is getting to know God your passion? Is it so important to you that, just as Jesus did for you, you're willing to make sacrifices to spend time with Him? When you are passionate about His purpose for your life, then you're willing to do whatever it takes to live for Him.

In Romans 15 the apostle Paul is clear—it is his ambition to bring the knowledge of Christ to everyone. Paul's dramatic encounter with Jesus on the road to Damascus changed his life radically. Knowing Jesus and sharing Him with others consumed Paul for the rest of his life.

The Word of God says, "He has also set eternity in the hearts of men; yet they cannot fathom what God has done from beginning to end" (Ecclesiastes 3:11). Often we think of eternity as a future event—our time in heaven—but eternity is *now*. As soon as you received Jesus as your Savior, you became a part of the eternal family of God. What you do today—what you invest your passion in—is a part of your eternal life.

As you discover your passion for the things of God, your desires for success and a meaningful life come full circle. You learn the true meaning of life.

Start living your forever life now, with a heart passionate for the things of God.

GROWING IN PASSION TOWARD GOD

God, I am growing in faith as I get to know You better. I know You first by what You have done for me. You have saved me from darkness and transformed me. You have given me purpose and meaning. Thank You for reaching down and changing my life. I want to become passionate about the things that are important to You. Teach me what I need to know to complete the destiny You have given me. Time with You is a delight as I get to know and understand Your will for my life.

PASSIONATE IN PRAYER

Father, I realize prayer is important for building a strong relationship with You. Jesus prayed constantly and consistently. People in relationships talk to one another. I never want to neglect my relationship with You. Help me to be faithful to You in prayer. I want to be open to hearing Your voice at all times.

A HOPEFUL VISION

Where there is no revelation, the people cast off restraint;
but happy is he who keeps the law.
PROVERBS 29:18 NKJV

Lord, we would surely perish if we didn't have the vision of Your plan for our lives. You brought us to this position, You supply us for our duties each day, and You will accomplish Your desire through us wherever we work. I thank You that I can trust You in the good times—when the job is going smoothly—as well as those times when Your design is less clear. Give me a vision, Lord—of You and of what You're accomplishing through me.

A WORTHY LIFE
As a prisoner for the Lord, then, I urge you to
live a life worthy of the calling you have received.
EPHESIANS 4:1

Lord Jesus, what an honor it is to be Your prisoner! I'm not locked up in jail as the apostle Paul often was, but I'm enslaved by love to You. You have called me to faith. I take that seriously and want to live a life worthy of You.

WHAT PLEASES GOD

God, I want to be passionate about the purpose You have for me. Show me the things in my life that please You and give me the courage and strength to pursue those things. Keep my purpose before me, fill my heart, and give me right motives to accomplish all You have set before me. As long as You are with me and my focus is on what pleases You, I cannot fail.

How much more shall the blood of Christ, who through the eternal Spirit offered Himself without spot to God, cleanse your conscience from dead works to serve the living God?
HEBREWS 9:14 NKJV

WHEN GOD SEEMS SILENT

God, forgive me for the times I walked away, too busy or self-absorbed to stay connected to You. I expect You to be upset with me, and I feel guilty, but Your love for me is unconditional. It's hard to trust when You are silent, but help me to do just that. And forgive me for the times when You were speaking and I wasn't listening. Help me to run to You instead of from You, so You can restore me to Yourself.

WHEN I'VE BEEN HURT

God, teach me to guard my heart above all else, because it determines the course of my life. I want to learn how to keep painful experiences from destroying me. I refuse to replay what happened over and over in my mind. Help me to let go of it. I don't want to think about the people involved, so help me to let them go by forgiving them. I ask You, Holy Spirit, to do a mighty work in my heart right now. Take what the enemy of my soul meant to harm me and turn it for my good.

FOR A RESTORED SOUL

Lord, in pursuit of what I thought should be my passion, my soul has been wounded. I am here to ask You for encouragement and strength. I'm not a quitter, but I need to make some major heart adjustments. Guide me with Your Word and speak to me through preaching and teaching. Show me how to ask for help, and bring people who love me and Your Word into my life to give me godly counsel.

STANDING UP FOR MY FAITH

Heavenly Father, I want to let my light shine before all people. Teach me to live and act in a way that speaks Your truth to others. Fill me with an undying passion to see lives changed for Your glory. When I'm called to defend my faith, help me to do it in love, with gentleness and respect.

Let the message about Christ, in all its richness, fill your lives. Teach and counsel each other with all the wisdom he gives. Sing psalms and hymns and spiritual songs to God with thankful hearts.
COLOSSIANS 3:16 NLT

FREEDOM FROM WRONG PASSIONS

God, I've been exposed to cultic or occult practices, false religions, and false teachers. I have sinned against You, and I feel so guilty. Help me to come boldly before Your throne of grace and accept Your forgiveness. Help me to forgive myself. Forgive me for accepting a counterfeit to the truth. Today I am letting go of wrong passions and embracing a stronger desire for You, Lord. I thought I was strong enough to be exposed to something like this—but I wasn't ready. Help me to separate myself immediately from any relationships that jeopardize my commitment to You.

CALLED ACCORDING TO HIS PURPOSE

[God] has saved us and called us with a holy calling, not according
to our works, but according to His own purpose and grace
which was granted us in Christ Jesus from all eternity.
2 TIMOTHY 1:9 NASB

Dear God, I thank You that our calling is not dependent upon
our own efforts, but upon Your purpose and the grace You gave
us in Jesus. Your purpose is never random, but something You've
planned for all time. I want to be one with Your plan—one with
You in Your eternal purpose of bringing people to know You.

OUR REAL CALLING

That you would walk worthy of God who
calls you into His own kingdom and glory.
1 THESSALONIANS 2:12 NKJV

Dear Lord, this is my true calling: walking worthily into Your
kingdom and glory. May I order my steps in such a way as to be
worthy of Your calling, spiritually and professionally. Help me,
Father, to show your life within me to the world outside. May it
be clear to those around me that You are the Lord of my life.

THE PURSUIT OF DILIGENCE

Lord, in all I do in pursuit of You, help me to be diligent. Help me to stay on task and accomplish my work faithfully and responsibly. No matter what work is set before me, I want to be motivated to do it as though I am doing it for You and not for others.

WHEN OVERCOME WITH COMPASSION FOR OTHERS

Lord, I appreciate You giving me sensitivity toward others. It makes me who I am. Yet, honestly, I am worn out from caring for others. There is so much drama in the lives of my friends and family members, and I can't give when I'm exhausted emotionally. Instruct me in Your wisdom as to who I should give my time to. Show me when and where to take time for myself. Help me to know when I need to stop giving to others and take care of myself.

WAITING ON GOD

My feet are positioned at the starting line. I'm ready to run the race. All I need now is Your signal for me to begin it. I believe I've found my passion and I'm ready to act on it, but I know I need to wait for Your timing. Help me to be patient. Alert me to what I still need to do in making my preparations.

I long, yes, I faint with longing to enter
the courts of the LORD. With my whole being,
body and soul, I will shout joyfully to the living God.
PSALM 84:2 NLT

FUEL FOR MY PASSION

Lord, I am beginning to discover my passion for the things that concern You. I am ready to embrace Your meaning for my life. You know what I need to fuel my passion. Make it come alive in my heart. There is a fire burning in my soul to do what You have called me to do. Set things in motion to help me achieve the dream You gave me. Help me to hold tight to this passion and never let the fire in my soul burn out.

MY PEACE—THE POWER OF CONTENTMENT

As I write this, it's snowing. A blizzard, actually. Although it's only late October, the winds are whipping and fourteen inches of snow are piling up on the lawn and lawn furniture. Inside the house, though, all is calm—because the sturdy walls protect me from the stormy blast. Content and safe by a warm fireplace, I am at peace.

Like a winter squall, the storms of life can threaten our inner peace. An unexpected job layoff or doctor's report can disrupt our emotional equilibrium. A hurtful comment from a neighbor or coworker can cut us. Even the daily duties of life—from diapers and dishes to deals and deadlines—leave us exhausted.

For most of us, life is busy—and the peace we find often seems short-lived. There is so much to think about—the kids, the mortgage, our health, and how we're ever going to find time to get everything done. Even contentment, when we find it, is fleeting. We get our dream jobs, our husbands surprise us with special vacations, our adult children finally find their own places to live. But with the flip of a calendar page, discontentment returns.

Why is peace so elusive? Perhaps because we forget to pray and replenish our source of peace. We can find lasting contentment in Christ, regardless of our circumstances, when we come to the One who calms the storms. "It is in the silence of the heart that God speaks," said Mother Teresa—but too often our hearts are neither still nor silent.

Peace rarely comes naturally; in most cases, we need to learn it. The true story of two sisters provides a good example: Mary, Martha, and their brother Lazarus (yes, the same guy Jesus raised from the dead) all lived in the town of Bethany. When Jesus came to visit, Martha scurried around preparing food while Mary took the opportunity to sit at Jesus' feet and absorb the enlightening things He said. That day, Mary made the better choice, because Jesus was not to be with them much longer. She had been wise and was rewarded for it. (You can read the whole story in Luke 10:38–42.)

In the midst of a frenzied life, though, we can find a refuge, a sanctuary of inner stillness, in drawing near to God. Powerful prayers for peace rise as we spend time in His presence, enjoying and resting in His capable strength. Just as the moon takes its light and power from the sun, we can bask in the glow of God's Son and absorb His truth. Then we'll be women who reflect His joy and light the dark corners of the world around us. Peace is possible when we seek the Source of peace through prayer.

BE A PEACEMAKER

Lord, please make me a tool of Your peace. Instead of the hammer of judgment, let me bring the balm of love. Instead of bitterness and resentment, help me to quickly forgive. When doubt misaligns my emotions, level me with faith. When I cannot find an answer, let me know Your great hope. When I cannot see the way, bring Your light to my darkness. When I am feeling low, bring me joy. Lord, let me receive all these things so I can console others and be a peacemaker. (Inspired by the Prayer of St. Francis.)

CALM MY ANXIOUS HEART

Lord, I don't want to be anxious about anything, but so often I am. I thank You that You understand. Right now, I release my burdens and cares to You. I give You my heavy heart and my flailing emotions. I ask that You calm me, despite all that is happening in my life. As I keep my thoughts, actions, and attitudes centered on Jesus, Your peace comes. I thank You for Your peace that settles on me even when I do not understand.

FINDING CONTENTMENT

But godliness with contentment is great gain.
1 TIMOTHY 6:6

Lord, please help me to find my contentment in You. I don't want to be defined by "stuff"—the things I own or what I do. May my greatest happiness in life be knowing who You are and who I am in Christ. May I treasure the simple things in life, those things that bring me peace. With Your grace, I rest secure. Like Mary, I choose to sit at Your feet. You, Lord, are my satisfaction.

THE PEACE THAT BRINGS LIFE

A heart at peace gives life to the body,
but envy rots the bones.
PROVERBS 14:30

Lord, I thank You for the peace that restores me mentally, emotionally, and physically. It is the peace that brings wholeness. When my heart is restless, my health suffers. But when I am at peace, You restore my entire body. I can breathe easier, I can relax, and I can smile again because I know everything's going to be all right. You are in control. I thank You that Your peace brings life.

A PEACEFUL LIFE

Lord, I don't want peace to be a once-in-a-while thing—I want to know peace as a way of life. Make me a conduit that brings harmony and serenity to all my relationships and interactions. Even when life is busy, I want to be a person who takes time to listen to others. Still my inner heart so I can give a smile or a kind word to another person and, through my actions, offer peace to them as well.

THE WISDOM OF PEACE

Lord, please plant Your wisdom in me like seeds in the soil. Each seed of wisdom is a gift from heaven. Help me cultivate each one and learn to follow Your ways. They are pure, peace-loving, considerate, submissive, full of mercy and good fruit, impartial, and sincere. May I be a person who sows in peace and raises a harvest of righteousness. As I look to Your Word for growth, teach me to meditate on it and apply it to my life.

WHERE IS PEACE FOUND?

For the kingdom of God is not a matter of eating and drinking, but of righteousness, peace and joy in the Holy Spirit, because anyone who serves Christ in this way is pleasing to God and approved by men.
ROMANS 14:17–18

Lord, everyone is looking for peace. Some travel to other countries or try alternative philosophies and lifestyles to find an inner tranquility. Some think food or wine will satisfy the hole in the heart that only You can fill. But Your Word tells us it's not what we eat or drink that provides lasting satisfaction. May I find peace and joy in Your Holy Spirit, Lord. Knowing You, loving You, and experiencing You is true peace. Thank You, Lord.

PEACE LIKE A RIVER

Lord, I need Your river of life to flow through me today. Wash away my cares and help me to follow as I learn to "go with the flow" of Your will. Still my restless heart with the grandeur of Your creation. I can imagine myself walking on a sandy shore, the ocean mist and rhythmic music of the waves revealing Your splendor. I appreciate all You have made. I thank You for the peace Your creation brings.

FOCUS ON GOD, NOT CIRCUMSTANCES

Lord, so many times it seems like a thief is trying to steal my peace. My circumstances can be overwhelming—and they shake me up. I don't want to be robbed of happiness and emotional stability. I ask that You would keep me in perfect peace as I choose to put my eyes on You, rather than my problems. Let my mind be steady, not racing. Let my heart trust that You will see me through.

A BLESSING OF PEACE

"The LORD bless you and keep you; the LORD make
his face shine upon you and be gracious to you;
the LORD turn his face toward you and give you peace."
NUMBERS 6:24–26

Lord, long ago You told Moses to have Aaron and his sons bless the Israelites with these words. I ask that You would bless me with peace as I pray: "The LORD bless you and keep you; the LORD make his face shine upon you and be gracious to you; the LORD turn his face toward you and give you peace." Turn to me, and let Your love and mercy shine on me so I can be a light that shines the way for others.

LEARNING THE WAYS OF PEACE

Lord, I am so grateful that You are helping me become a person who walks in peace. Mentor me in Your ways so I can live in harmony and be a positive example for others. I don't want to put anyone down; I want to build them up. I don't want to start fights or nag people; I want to bring them happiness. Instead of putting myself first, let me be considerate of others. Forgive me if I have been proud or arrogant; teach me, Lord, to be humble.

NOT AS THE WORLD GIVES

Lord, Your peace is unlike anything that the world offers. I don't need to upgrade to a new model every year—there's no "Peace 5.0" to download. I have the only version I need when I have Your peace, whether that's a calm tranquility, a quiet stillness, or the inner knowledge that everything's going to be all right. I value my right standing with You and the harmony that brings to my relationships. Your peace is real and lasting, never to be taken away.

PEACE WITH OTHERS

Live in peace with each other.
1 THESSALONIANS 5:13

Lord, I need Your peace today. Some people are just hard to be around. They talk too much or seem too needy. Our personalities rub each other the wrong way. God, I need the power of Your Holy Spirit to stay calm. I don't want to be frustrated or lose my temper. I want to be at peace around others—even the people who so differ from me. Impart in me Your loving ways so I can be at peace with others.

REST ASSURED

"Be still, and know that I am God; I will be exalted among the nations, I will be exalted in the earth."
PSALM 46:10

Lord, I thank You for the gift of Your peace and contentment in my life. You are awesome! I am learning that I can be at peace because You have a plan. You can handle anything—even my entire life. You are sovereign, powerful, and wise—and You never drop the ball. Because of who You are, I can be still and rest assured, confident no matter what comes my way. Thank You, Lord.

WE ARE OVERCOMERS

Lord, our world is filled with trouble and pain—from the abuse, crime, and terrorism I see on the news to the drugs, affairs, and pornography addictions I hear about from people I know. Sometimes it seems like too much to handle. I am so glad that I have You, Lord. In this world there is trouble, but with You—being connected to You—I can have peace.

JESUS, PRINCE OF PEACE

Lord, I thank You that I can have a calm spirit—because You are the Prince of Peace. Your name, Jesus, has the authority to make fear and worry flee. Your name has power! You are called Wonderful Counselor because You freely give wisdom and guidance. You are the Mighty God, the One who made the entire world and keeps it all going. My Everlasting Father, it's Your love and compassion that sustain me. My Prince of Peace, I worship and honor You.

MY PERSONAL HISTORY—
THE POWER OF TRANSFORMATION

On a late December day, a ten-year-old girl makes a cheery snowman with her friends. After they leave, she stays outside just a bit longer, soaking in the last moments of play and watching the afternoon fade to twilight. She listens to the wind blowing through the towering oak trees around her, and the silence that follows. In the quiet stillness, she smiles. She is happy.

As I look back on that innocent childhood memory—a piece of my personal history—I never could have imagined that day how my world would change. A few years later my parents would divorce, and I would move to another town—and then another. My spirit then could not have comprehended the devastating effect of a family member's coming illness, or of breakups between significant others. On the other hand, I could not have expected how wonderful it would be to hold a newborn niece, or to live in the majestic splendor of the Rocky Mountain foothills. On that winter day, I didn't know that the best thing to come into my life was just around the corner—and His name was Jesus.

We all have a past. We smile over some recollections. But while many memories are happy, others hurt. We have sometimes suffered abandonment, abuse, or tragedy, and we're still harboring hurt and anger.

Though we can't change what has happened, we can change our perspective. With the power of prayer we can learn from our past, find healing, and be thankful for the good times God gives.

The Samaritan woman we meet in John 4 had a past she wanted to hide. She had been married five times—and was living with a sixth man who was not her husband. When she met Jesus near a well at midafternoon, she was surprised that He already knew everything about her. Despite her ugly history, He offered her a beautiful future. "As far as Jesus is concerned, the woman with no future has a future; the woman with a string of failures is about to have the string broken. Jesus sees her present desire, which makes her past irrelevant," says Michael Yaconelli in *Messy Spirituality.* "Jesus can redeem our past, no matter what kind of past we bring with us: failure, mistakes, bad decisions, immaturity, and even a past which was done to us."

Whether we're the ones who messed up or someone else wounded us, we can give our past to God in prayer. He is able to redeem it. We can experience healing from hurt and release from pain.

It's a mystery how that transformation happens—but when we pray about our yesterdays, we can find healing for today and hope for our tomorrows.

RETURNING TO THE LORD

Lord, some of the things in my past have led me far from You. I want to come back and be in right standing with You again. I ask for forgiveness for the things I have done wrong—in both my distant past and more recently. I am so glad that You are gracious and compassionate. Thank You for being slow to anger and abounding in love. Here I am, Lord; I return to You.

WE NEED TO REMEMBER

Lord, I want to remember the good things You have done for me in the past. Like the stones the Israelites took out of the Jordan River, I need my own personal "rocks of remembrance" of Your mercies in my life. You performed miracles for them—allowing them to cross the river on dry ground, parting the Red Sea for them—so that people today might know Your powerful hand. As I recall the ways You have helped me throughout my life, I honor You.

LETTING GO OF THE PAST

My eyes are ever on the LORD, for only
he will release my feet from the snare.
PSALM 25:15

Lord, it's hard to let go of things that are comfortable and familiar, even when they're not good for me anymore. I need Your strong power to release my grasp, finger by finger, on the things I cling to so tightly—like unhealthy ways of thinking or relationships that are not bearing fruit. As I release them to You, give me the courage to receive all You have waiting for my empty, trusting hands.

OVERCOMING OPPRESSION

Lord, I ask for Your strong power to heal me from oppression. I pray against evil and for good. I pray the shed blood of Jesus over my life. Keep me safe and protected. There is nothing, no single thing, that can keep me from you—neither death nor life, neither angels nor demons, neither the present nor the future, nor any powers, neither height nor depth, nor anything else in all creation. Cover me, Lord, and be near me today.

LIVING IN THE PRESENT

Lord, I have been camping in the past too long. Pull up my tent stakes and help me to move on. There is so much to live for today! The past is over and the future awaits. Today I choose to worship you, my Lord and Maker. When I hear Your voice, may my heart be soft—not hardened or jaded by the past. Today is a gift; I celebrate the present with You, Lord.

LEARNING FROM THE PAST

Not only so, but we also rejoice in our sufferings,
because we know that suffering produces perseverance;
perseverance, character; and character, hope.
ROMANS 5:3–4

Lord, I thank You for Your patience as I learn important lessons from my past. I don't want to repeat my mistakes, Lord. Your ways are not our ways, but Your ways are best. They bring healing and life. As I learn to rejoice in the suffering I've experienced, I can see Your hand teaching me perseverance; from perseverance I develop character, and from character I have hope.

MOVING PAST MY MISTAKES

God, You don't speak to me according to my past mistakes, and my heavenly rewards are not based on how many times I have failed or succeeded. Although I can't erase my past, You can—and have. Thank You for removing my transgressions and filling me with Your great love and kindness in exchange. Help me to learn from my past and to move forward.

"The thief comes only to steal and kill and destroy;
I have come that they may have life, and have it to the full."
JOHN 10:10

LETTING GO OF RESENTMENT

Lord, You know my feelings of resentment against certain people. Forgive me for feeling this way. I won't waste any more time or energy on this. I am only hurting myself by holding on to resentment. Help me to let go of the hurt and anger I feel. I don't want to hold grudges. I don't want this to have power over me any longer. I release it to You. You forgave me and I choose to forgive them. I have no more desire for revenge. Help me to love them with the love You have shared with me.

WHEN I'VE COMPROMISED

Lord, thank You for showing me that the greatest danger to my faith can be when I'm tempted to compromise. Truth isn't negotiable, and I want to be on the side of truth. I don't want to compromise the character, nature, or values that come with my life in Christ. When I do, my old nature leads me instead of Your Spirit. Forgive me and help me to stay the course. Guide me in Your truth so I can stand strong, unwilling to compromise.

COURAGE TO ASK OTHERS FOR FORGIVENESS

God, it is hard to go to others and ask them to forgive me. I can think of all kinds of excuses why I don't have to apologize. The truth is, it's so humbling and embarrassing. Help me to swallow my pride. Give me courage to go to them and be authentic and genuine about my feelings. Help me to face their disappointment, anger, and hurt. Give me words that will help heal our hearts and put things right again, if possible. Teach me to be accountable to others with my words and actions.

FORGIVENESS FOR THE UNFORGIVABLE SIN

Father, I feel my sin should be unforgivable. I thought it was the answer to my problems, but since then it's been torturing my mind. The Bible says sin is sin—no matter how small or how big. And I know when I ask for forgiveness, You throw my sin into a sea of forgetfulness and never remember it again. I give You this sin today and I let it go. I refuse to let my past torture me anymore. Thank You for forgiving me and surrounding me with Your love.

WHEN I'VE BLAMED GOD

God, I've experienced a deep hurt and I didn't know who to blame, so I blamed You. I guess I felt You should have protected me or prevented it from happening. I was just so grieved that I couldn't see the truth. Now I know it wasn't Your fault. Help me to understand what happened. Forgive me for running away from You instead of to You. Thank You for welcoming me into Your open arms even when I was pushing You away. I'm so glad You never gave up on me.

CHANGE ME, LORD

Yet, O LORD, you are our Father. We are the clay,
you are the potter; we are all the work of your hand.
ISAIAH 64:8

Lord, You know all about me—my past, my present, and my future. You are the Potter and I am the clay, the work of Your hands. As You reshape my life, changing me from who I was and molding me into the woman You want me to be, help me to trust Your wisdom. I want to be a vessel sturdy enough to hold all the love You have for me—and to pour that out on others.

TRUTH SETS YOU FREE

To the Jews who had believed him, Jesus said, "If you
hold to my teaching, you are really my disciples. Then you
will know the truth, and the truth will set you free."
JOHN 8:31–32

Lord, I am free! Finally! For so long I was bound in sin, selfishness, and unhealthy ways of thinking. I tried to change on my own, but like a prisoner in handcuffs I was powerless; I could not break free on my own. Praise You, Lord—You loosed the chains that held me. Your love and strength empowered me, Lord. I choose to stay on Your path and follow the way of freedom. Your truth sets me free!

THE ULTIMATE GIFT

Lord, thank You for the greatest gift—forgiveness. I am honored to be a recipient of Your mercy. It's a gift I want to share with others. Help me to learn to forgive others easily. You are my example. When I'm tempted to react to the things that hurt and offend me, remind me of Your willingness to forgive me. Teach me to see things from others' perspectives. Give me a heart of compassion so I freely give others the ultimate gift that You have shared with me.

SECOND CHANCES

God, You are the God of second chances. Today as I confess my guilt and admit my sins, You are faithful to give me a fresh start. Your mercies are new every morning. Thank You for changing my life by the power of Your heavenly pardon.

MY PRAISES—
THE POWER OF THANKSGIVING AND ADORATION

What a privilege to approach God, to bow down before Him, laud Him with our praises, and feel His presence within us! Sometimes, as we draw near, appropriate words evade us. Yet all is not lost, for God has given us a powerful, praise-filled resource—the book of Psalms. Richard J. Foster wrote, "The Psalms are the literature of worship and their most prominent feature is praise. 'Praise the Lord!' is the shout that reverberates from one end of the Psalter to the other. Singing, shouting, dancing, rejoicing, adoring—all are the language of praise."

As we spend time praising our Lord and Savior, our lives are transformed in several ways. First and foremost, our spirits become intimately connected with His. As we lift our voices, extolling His name and deeds, we are invaded by His presence. "But You are holy, O You Who dwell in [the holy place where] . . .praises. . .[are offered]" (Psalm 22:3 AMP). God abides within us when we praise Him!

Second, when we praise God our fears are allayed. Psalm 56:10–11 says, "In God, whose word I praise, in the Lord, whose word I praise—in God I trust; I will not be afraid." There is no room for fear where praise has taken up residence.

Third, praise changes our outlook as we view our world through the eyes of our Creator. "Praise the Lord from the heavens. . . . Let [His angels, heavenly hosts, sun, moon, stars, highest heavens, waters above the skies] praise the name of the Lord, for he commanded and they were created" (Psalm 148:1, 5). Suddenly, when we see things from the perspective of the One who made and sustains the entire universe, the cares of this world grow dim.

Fourth, praise vanquishes our enemy. Second Chronicles 20 tells the story of when Jehoshaphat, king of Judah, was faced with a vast army coming against him. He prayed to the Lord, "We do not know what to do, but our eyes are upon you" (v. 12). The people bowed down and worshipped the Lord. The next morning, Jehoshaphat appointed his men to sing to the Lord and praise His name. They went out into the front lines, ahead of the army, saying, "Give thanks to the LORD, for his love endures forever" (v. 21). The result? Not only was that day's foe vanquished (the enemy armies ended up destroying each other), but for the remainder of Jehoshaphat's reign, "God [gave] him rest on every side" (v. 30).

And finally, our love for God is deepened when we adore Him and give Him thanks for past blessings. It is then we are reminded that "for as high as the heavens are above the earth, so great is his love for those who fear him" (Psalm 103:11).

After the sun rises but before you approach God with your daily petitions, get into the praise mode, reminding Him (and yourself) how terrific He really is, how awed you are to have Him in your life, how blessed you are that He came down to earth to save *you*. Drench yourself in the words of praise amid the Psalms. Sing a familiar worship song at the top of your lungs! Have no reservations as you come into His presence, glorifying His name. And as you speak to your Creator, through His Word, He will speak to you.

SHOUTING FOR JOY!

Your hands created the heavens and the earth. You breathed upon Adam and gave him life. Everything that was created was created through Your Son, Jesus Christ. The trees, the earth, the waters, and the creatures clap their hands in praise to You. This is the day that You have made! I will rejoice and be glad in it as I shout Your name to the heavens!

PRAISING IN SONG

My heart rejoices in Your presence this morning! To Your ears, Lord, I pray that my singing will be a joyful noise. Your grace is amazing. You are my all in all; I worship and adore You. Lean down Your ear to me as I sing about Your love, for how great Thou art, Lord! How great Thou art!

AN ANSWER TO MY CRY

Dear God, You have done so many things for me, saved me from so many dangers, toils, and snares. I cry out to You again this morning. Fill me with Your Spirit. Touch me with Your presence. And as I go through this day, may I be so filled with Your praises that I cannot help but tell others what You have done for me!

BY HIS GREAT MERCY

Lord, I humble myself before You, bowing down at Your throne. You are so great, so awesome. Your presence fills this universe. I am filled with Your amazing love, touched by Your compassion. There is no one like You in my life, my Master, my Lord, my God.

PRAISE SILENCES ENEMIES

From the lips of children and infants you have ordained praise
because of your enemies, to silence the foe and the avenger.
PSALM 8:2

With You on my side—You who hold the heavens in Your hands,
You who sustain the entire universe—I need not be afraid of my
enemies, of those who wish to harm me, or of the evil one who
dogs my steps. With praises to You on my lips and in my heart,
my foes are vanquished. You are my great refuge, my rock of
strength.

HIS AWESOME POWER

Say to God, "How awesome are your deeds! So great
is your power. . . . All the earth bows down to you;
they sing praise to you, they sing praise to your name."
PSALM 66:3–4

Lord, You parted the Red Sea and You still the wind and the
waves. You give sight to the blind and hearing to the deaf. You
raise people from the dead. Your power is awesome. Nothing is
impossible for You. I bow before You, singing praises to Your
name.

PRAISE FOR DELIVERANCE

You are the Good Shepherd, the All-Sufficient One, my Rock of Refuge. You hold the universe in Your hands, and yet You are concerned with everything going on in my life. I am staggered by Your love and faithfulness to me. You continually draw me up into Your presence. You deliver me from the depths of darkness.

NO FEAR WHEN GOD IS NEAR

Your instruction keeps me on the right path, and for that I praise You. Thank You for giving me Your Holy Word, to have and to hold. With Your Word I can speak to You and You can speak to me. You are the Great Communicator of my life. I trust in Your Word, for when I am armed with it, I have no fear.

HEART-FILLED PRAISE

As I sit here before You, my heart reaches out to touch You, the great God, seated in the heavens. Meld my spirit with Yours so that our wills are one. Your love and faithfulness are tremendous. I praise You, Lord, with my lips, my voice, my mouth, my life.

LIFELONG PRAISE

At this moment and throughout this day, I sing my praises to You, O God. Music is one of Your gifts, and I thank You for it. As my spirit in song rises to join with Yours, may I continually be reminded of all You are, all You have done, and all You will do.

PRAISE TO THE HEAVENLY CREATOR

Bless the LORD, O my soul! O LORD my God, You are very great:
You are clothed with honor and majesty, who cover Yourself with
light as with a garment, who stretch out the heavens like a curtain.
He lays the beams of His upper chambers in the waters, who makes
the clouds His chariot, who walks on the wings of the wind.
PSALM 104:1–3 NKJV

You made all the planets, all the stars, the waters on the earth,
the land on which I stand. Is there nothing too difficult for You?
You are wrapped in light, and I come now into that light, to be
with You, to revel in Your presence, to praise Your holy name.
Surround me with Your arms among these clouds.

PRAISE FOR FORGIVENESS AND HEALING

Let all that I am praise the LORD; may I never forget the good things
he does for me. He forgives all my sins and heals all my diseases.
PSALM 103:2–3 NLT

Dear Lord, You have given Your one and only Son to die for me.
Because of You and Your great gift, I have eternal life. You have
forgiven my sins and healed my soul. Nothing is impossible with
You in my life. Thank You for taking care of me. With all that I
am, with my entire being, I praise You forever and ever!

IN HIM IS VICTORY

Lord, You are worthy of all my adoration. I'm amazed at how much I am blessed when I praise You. When I'm glorifying You, I feel Your strength. I know You are with me in a special way. I want my entire existence to be centered on You, for You are awesome. Without You my life would lie in shattered ruins, but You give me victory.

ALL YE PEOPLE

Thank You, Lord, that all people are important to You. Thank You that even I am instructed to praise You. You've done so much for me every day of my life. You give me strength and breath. You meet all my needs abundantly. You've blessed me with a beautiful family. The list goes on and on and is topped by the gift of Your precious Son. I cannot help but praise You.

PRAISE FOR STRENGTH

To You, O my Strength, I will sing praises;
for God is my defense, my God of mercy.
PSALM 59:17 NKJV

When I am weak, Your strength upholds me. When I am afraid, Your courage sustains me. When I am downcast, Your presence lifts me. You are always there for me. How great, how wonderful, how amazing You are, my God, my Friend, my Father. I am here before You, singing endless praises to Your name!

PRAISE FOR HIS GIFTS!

I am in high spirits today, Lord. You have provided all that I need and more! Along with my earthly needs, You have provided me with grace, spiritual gifts, love, forgiveness, Your Word, Your Son. My heart is so light. I come to You singing praises, and I leave with a smile on my lips. In Your presence, my spirit is lifted. Praise the Lord!

MY RELATIONSHIPS—THE POWER OF FORGIVENESS

Relationships—between you and God, you and yourself, and you and others—can be a fragile thing. And when such relationships are breached, you can be sure the bane of unforgiveness is at the core.

Forgiving those who offend us is difficult at best. The more heinous the infraction, the harder it is to pardon the perpetrator. Yet that is exactly what Jesus calls us to do. Granted, forgiving someone who murders your child is much harder than forgiving the individual who speaks ill of you. But words can be as sharp as the blade of a killer's knife. It amazes me how family squabbles can keep siblings and other family members from talking to one another for the rest of their lives—or how one careless word from a friend can sever a lifelong relationship.

It has been said that refusing to forgive someone who injures you is like drinking poison and expecting the offender to die. David Jeremiah wrote, "The only way to heal the pain that will not heal itself is to forgive the person who hurt you. Forgiving heals your memory as you change your memory's vision. When you release the wrongdoer from your wrath, you cut a malignant tumor out of your own life. You set a prisoner free. . .and discover that the prisoner you freed was yourself."

But if we know there is such freedom in forgiveness, why does it seem so hard? We must ask ourselves, "If Jesus can be stripped naked, beaten, scourged, have nails driven into his hands and feet, hang on a cross until death, and still say, 'Father, forgive them, for they do not know what they are doing' (see Luke 23:34), why can't we?" "Oh well," you say, "it was easy for Him. He was God." Yet God insists we forgive others no matter how big or small the offenses. But how do we tap into His power of forgiveness?

The first step is to allow yourself to feel the hurt of the offenses against you, both past and present. Pray for the release of that hurt, and then pray for the power to forgive as God constantly and consistently forgives you. Continue to pray until you have truly forgiven in your heart. (It may not happen immediately, but it *will* happen.) Then thank God for His goodness and peace. Finally, when the time is right, try to restore your relationship with the person who hurt you. Pray for the right words to say. Someone has to be willing to take the first step—and that someone is you. All the while, keep in mind that, although your offender's behavior may not change, you will, becoming more like Christ!

If you have offended yourself or God, talk to Him, pouring out your heart. Ask for His forgiveness, and then try to do better the next time. Don't constantly berate yourself for your bad behavior, toward either yourself or others. God does not forgive us based on how well we perform or how acceptable we believe we are in His sight. He forgives us based on the sacrifice of Jesus Christ. Oswald Chambers wrote, "Forgiveness means not merely that I am saved from sin and made right for heaven . . . . Forgiveness means that I am forgiven into a recreated relationship, into identification with God in Christ."

Don't poison yourself with the bitter pill of *unforgiveness*—it's suicide! Instead, tap into the power of *forgiveness*, keeping Jesus' peace in your mind, His mercy in your heart, His power at hand, and your relationships whole.

TWO-WAY FORGIVENESS

It's a two-way street, Lord—we forgive others and then You will forgive us. I know I've read that scripture a hundred times, but I've never understood it more fully than today. Give me the strength of Your forgiveness this morning, Lord. Help me to love and not hate the person who has hurt me. Thank You for releasing the poison of unforgiveness that has been building up within me.

FORGIVING MY FRIEND

I've about had it, Lord. I keep getting hurt by my friend. I don't know how much more of this I can take! Is this friendship even worth all this pain? Lord, please calm me down. Give me the right attitude. Your Word says that no matter how many times I am offended, if my friend apologizes and says she'll never do it again, I am to forgive her. Well, You're going to have to give me this power, because I have none left of my own. Please work, live, and love through me. Help me to forgive my friend.

WHEN I'VE JUDGED OTHERS

Jesus, please forgive me for judging others. I hate it when others judge me, but it's so easy to condemn, categorize, and criticize the choices others make. Forgive me for being close-minded, opinionated, self-righteous, and unloving toward the very people You gave Your life for. They are valuable and precious to You. Teach me to see them that way, too. Help me to allow others to express their thoughts and opinions without feeling that my own beliefs are under attack. It is not my place to judge anyone. If possible, let me bring them Your truth in love.

A CLEAN HEART

When people look at my life, I want them to see a heart full of truth. Help me to let go of the hurts hidden deep within my heart. Help me to remove the ugly, hurtful traces of who I used to be and to reveal who You have helped me become. I want a changed heart. I want to be filled with Your goodness, mercy, and love. I want to become a mirror, reflecting Your image to those around me.

EASILY OFFENDED

Lord, I have such anger within me for all the wrongs done to me all day long. Even when I'm out in traffic and someone cuts me off, I'm really miffed. Or when my family comes to the dinner table and no one appreciates how hard I've worked to make this meal but complains about every little thing, I just want to scream! Give me that new heart. Empty this heart of stone, the one so easily offended. Fill it with Your love.

NO GUILT TRIPS, PLEASE

I don't know why, Lord, but I just keep bringing up old offenses and throwing them into the faces of those who have hurt me. I know that's not how You want me to behave. If I keep on this course, there's no telling how many people I will alienate from my life. And I'm not being a very good example of a Christian. Help me to forgive others and not remind them of past deeds. Help me to pour out Your love to all.

SPREADING THE POWER OF FORGIVENESS

Lord, when Peter denied You three times, he wept bitterly. I know just how he felt. But You *knew* that's what he was going to do, and You gave him words to keep him from wallowing in self-pity. You told Peter to strengthen his brethren after he turned back to You. So I come before You this morning, asking You to forgive me and help me to forgive myself. Then, Lord, give me the opportunity to strengthen others who are dealing with unforgiveness. Help me encourage them to reconcile with those whom they have hurt or who have hurt them. All for Your glory, Lord.

NEEDING MERCY

Lord, I am so mad at myself. I have been doing wrong and hiding it from everyone. I even imagined I could hide it from You, but You know all. Lord, please forgive me for not admitting my sins to You. Help me to do better. I don't want to live this way. Sometimes I can't stand myself. Please help me to turn from this behavior. Give me Your never-ending mercy and eternal loving-kindness.

FORGIVE AND FORGET

Why can't I forgive and forget, Lord? Please help me forgive the person who injured me the other day. Instill in me Your power, Your grace, and Your mercy. With each breath I take in Your presence, I feel that power growing within me. Thank You, Lord. Now, please give me the means to forget this pain. I don't want to keep bringing it up and picking at the wound. Help me, Lord, as weak as I am, to forgive the offender and forget the pain.

NO ROOM FOR THE EVIL ONE

When I can't forgive, when I can't control my anger, I know I am giving the devil a foothold into my relationships and situations. And that is not a good thing. Help me to be a forgiving person, looking for healing and reconciliation instead of fostering bitterness and retribution. You are my life and my light. Forgive me for my attitude last night and give me Your love and power today.

HOLDING THAT TONGUE

Whenever I bring up past deeds, I start the cycle of pain all over again. Why do I do that, Lord? Please stop me! Help me to hold my tongue, to think before I speak. Change my thoughts to those of Christ. Help me to think of the good things, the good times, I have shared with my offenders. And if there weren't any good times, remind me that You love them just as much as You love me. Help me to put their need for forgiveness above my pride. Give me Your power to live this life and be the person You want me to be.

QUICK FORGIVENESS

You have chosen me to be Your child. Help me to live that life dressed in Your love. I need Your kindness, humility, quiet strength, discipline, and definitely Your even temper. Help me to forgive others quickly and not let bitterness rot my soul. I want to forgive others as quickly as You forgive us. Thank You for the gift of forgiveness. Adorn me with Your love today and every day!

WHEN I FEEL BETRAYED

Jesus, I know You experienced betrayal when Judas kissed You in the garden. What I am experiencing can't compare, but it brings me comfort knowing that You understand. I am hurt and feel so deceived. How can I open myself up and learn to trust someone again? Help me to heal quickly and forgive without compromising myself.

> *It is no longer I who live, but Christ lives in me.*
> *So I live in this earthly body by trusting in the*
> *Son of God, who loved me and gave himself for me.*
> GALATIANS 2:20 NLT

THE BENEFITS OF FORGIVENESS

Heavenly Father, thank You for forgiving me and removing the shame of my sin from me. With all I've done, I am thankful You choose not to hold anything against me. Through Your forgiveness I can enjoy the freedom of Your blessings. And I can forgive myself because You have forgiven me.

WHEN I'M FEELING GUILTY

Father, You gave me a fresh start when I received Your gift of salvation, but memories of my past sins find their way to the front of my mind. Remind me that You have wiped the slate clean. My past no longer exists for You. Relieve me of this pressure of guilt—my sin is gone! I let go of it today and refuse to let old memories enslave me. I give them all to You. Help me to create new memories of Your goodness and love for me. Thank You for setting me free.

> *"I will be merciful to their unrighteousness, and their sins and their lawless deeds I will remember no more."*
> HEBREWS 8:12 NKJV

FORGIVE ME FOR FAKING IT

Jesus, I've been talking Christian-ese. I've learned all the right things to say in front of people. They think I'm so spiritual, but I'm lost in the rules of religion. Forgive me for faking it. I desire to have a real relationship with You. Consume me with Your presence. I don't care what others think; my relationship is about You and only You!

MY RESPONSIBILITIES—THE POWER OF COMMITMENT

Have you ever been disappointed when someone didn't follow through on a commitment they made to you? When someone you trust makes a promise to you, you normally build an expectation to see that promise through. Do you keep every promise you make? Are you responsible for your actions and words?

You can count on God to keep His promises and commitments. Our very world—the earth we walk, the air we breathe, and the water that sustains us—was created by His Word. God's Word holds everything together, and if the devil could get God to break His Word, just one time, all creation would cease to exist.

You are created in God's image, and your word has power. The more you protect your word and do what you say you will do, the more power your word has in your life and in the lives of those who trust you. Do you disappoint others with promises you can't keep? Excuses are just that—excuses. No matter how valid those excuses are, others will remember whether or not you followed through on your commitment.

You need people you can count on to keep their commitments, and your family and friends need to be able to count on you when you take on responsibility. They need to know you're going to deliver. And God needs to know that He can count on you, too.

Responsible people know the importance of counting the cost before they make a commitment. They count the cost.

The book of Esther is a beautiful story of a young woman who counted the cost. She knew she could die if she approached the king without him first summoning her, but still she took action at the risk of her own life to save her people.

Jesus told us to count the cost before we build (Luke 14:28). Every day you build your life. You add to or take away from who you are becoming. Any responsibility you take on should be considered carefully before you commit to it. Ask yourself what it's going to cost if you do it, and what it's going to cost if you don't. There's always a cost—spiritually, emotionally, relationally, financially, and even physically.

Ask God to help you count the cost and, with His direction, commit to the things that will add to your life here on earth today and for all eternity.

KEEPING PROMISES TO MYSELF

Lord, You created me for a specific purpose. I make promises to myself and think it's okay not to keep them. Help me to remember that I'm responsible to You for how my life turns out. Help me to keep the commitments I've set and give me the courage to accomplish them. Remind me that it's okay to do good things for myself that help me to become the person You created me to be.

For we are each responsible for our own conduct.
GALATIANS 6:5 NLT

MAKING REALISTIC COMMITMENTS

Father, I want to live a balanced life. I am tired of people pulling at me. Show me how to choose what is important and necessary. Give me strength to say no when something doesn't belong on my list. I can't do everything that is asked of me. Help me to see what's important and when it's important. I want to remain stable in my spiritual, physical, emotional, relational, and financial needs. Teach me how to negotiate my time and energy—leaving plenty of time for rest and fun while doing what is necessary in all the other areas of my life.

SOW, WATER, INCREASE

Lord, when I read exploits of New Testament disciples and modern-day missionaries, I realize my efforts pale in comparison to theirs. I take comfort that I can bring Your love to others through my present position and daily activities. I can sow a seed here and there through open and honest concern for others. I can encourage spiritual growth by living my life so others see Christian principles at work. I pray I will look for opportunities to open others' hearts to accept salvation.

PERSONAL RESPONSIBILITY

Lord, give me a sense of personal responsibility for the lost. I pray I can overcome irrational concerns that keep me from doing those things I know I should do. Give me courage that dominates my fears. Teach me ways I can bless others. Strengthen my decision to lead others to You. May I progress from my home to my neighbors to my extended family. Almighty God, I surrender myself to Your service.

WHEN I'M TEMPTED TO TAKE SHORTCUTS

God, people around me take moral shortcuts, but I know that isn't right for me. You have given me values of honor, integrity, and truth. Help me not to compromise. Although others may act without integrity as they climb the corporate ladder, it's not worth the price of my relationship with You to follow their example. You bless me because I choose what is right and just. Thank You for reminding me of the way I need to go.

WHEN I'M AFRAID TO COMMIT

I'm standing at a four-way stop. I don't know what to do. I have a huge decision in front of me but it means a high level of commitment. There's so much pressure to make a decision while I don't have all the facts. I'm conflicted and confused, but Your Word says that confusion is not of You. Help me to press through all the confusing clutter of this situation. Shine Your light on it and show me what You want me to do. Then if it's right, I'll do whatever it takes to be accountable, to see this thing through.

WHEN I BREAK A PROMISE

I did it again—I failed; I broke a promise. I feel guilty and ashamed. I thought I could pull it off but I've hurt someone and disappointed myself and You. Forgive me for not counting the cost and thinking I could manage this alone. Give me the courage to apologize and correct my mistake, whatever it takes. Please comfort the people I hurt and help them to forgive me and maybe let me try again.

Good people will be guided by honesty;
dishonesty will destroy those who are not trustworthy.
PROVERBS 11:3 NCV

COMMITMENT TO PRAYER

I get so busy with so many things that I often lose track of time and forget about You. Forgive me. I'm so sorry. I know You wait patiently for me to spend time with You. I'm asking You to remind me, prompt me, call to me. I promise to be more diligent with my time with You. You know everything there is to know about me. You hold all the answers for my life in the palm of Your hand. Help me to come to You, sit at Your feet, and listen carefully to the answers You have for my life questions.

KEEPING COMMITMENTS TO FRIENDS

I don't mean to take advantage of others, but I've done it. Forgive me for it. Jesus, open my eyes to see that I hurt my friends when I'm late, cancel, or just don't show up. Let me see this before it's too late to keep my commitments. Teach me how to schedule for interruptions and still keep the appointments that are most important on the schedule.

You yourself must be an example to them by doing good works of every kind. Let everything you do reflect the integrity and seriousness of your teaching. Teach the truth so that your teaching can't be criticized. Then those who oppose us will be ashamed and have nothing bad to say about us.
TITUS 2:7–8 NLT

KEEPING COMMITMENTS AT WORK

Jesus, some people on my team are difficult to work with. Their ideas are different and their values are questionable, yet we have to succeed together. I have commitments to them that are hard to keep. Help me to represent You on the team. Show me how to fulfill my commitments by Your standards. Help me to serve my team members as You would serve them. Remind me that we succeed or fail only as a team.

ENLISTING THE HELP OF OTHERS

Lord, why is it so hard sometimes to ask for help? I don't want people to think I'm weak or that the task is too hard. Change my perception of needing help. Give me a new understanding: asking for help doesn't mean I am weak, but that I value relationship with others. It says that I have confidence in their ability to assist me. Even when I need help from strangers, give me the courage to ask and to handle the rejection if they say no. Grant me approval by those I ask for help.

COUNTING THE COST

Everything I do or don't do costs me something—time, effort, emotional energy. When I choose, Lord, help me find balance. Will this added responsibility add to my life, add value to my relationships, or help me to achieve a higher standard of living at the cost of my health? Give me a reality check with each commitment I consider making.

CHOSEN TO SERVE

Father, at an assembly of the church, I expect to be renewed, strengthened, and aligned with Your will. I understand that to reach those goals, I must assist others and accept those assignments for which I've been chosen to serve. Often, Lord, I can find excuses for avoiding my obligations. Help me understand that when I neglect these opportunities to serve, I'm also neglecting my spiritual growth.

KEEPING FIT

Lord, because of my sedentary job, I must take the time to exercise to stay in shape. Unused muscles go slack. Only a good, well-directed exercise program will keep me healthy. I realize that if I don't work at it, my spiritual life will become weak, too. Should I become slack in reading Your Word, praying, and thinking upon spiritual truths, I will become spiritually feeble. Help me make time for spiritual strengthening.

NO MORE EXCUSES

When I refuse to accept personal responsibility, I create my own problems. Lord, forgive me when I blame others for my situation instead of taking necessary steps to change my circumstances. Help me to accept my mistakes, look at them realistically, and learn from them. Help me find the courage in You to embrace my personal responsibility and see it as an opportunity to grow. Give me strength to make responsible choices. Guide me with Your wisdom in all I do and help me see the truth of my actions clearly.

GOD'S COMMITMENT TO ME

Lord, You are great! I want the whole world to know what You have done for me. You have changed my life and set me free. I was lost and alone, and You found me. Everything I need is in You. You created me and crowned me with Your glory. You take responsibility for me, whether I succeed or fail. From the beginning of time, every promise You have made, You have kept. Generation after generation depends on You, just as I do.

MY SALVATION—THE POWER TO RESCUE MY SOUL

Salvation as a general term means "deliverance from destruction." The word comes from the same root as the word *salvage*, meaning "to save the cargo of a ship sunk by a storm at sea." As Christians, we view salvation as the rescuing of the soul from the shipwreck of sin. Pride, selfishness, and a self-righteous attitude can lead us into a sin-filled lifestyle. If we walk our self-directed course, we separate ourselves from God. We become so far from Him that we lose sight of Him. Problems arise that are beyond our ability to cope with—sickness, grief, injustice, destructive dependencies, or emotional turmoil. If we are wise and recognize that we have lost our way, we call for rescue. God alone can rescue us, but we have separated ourselves from His holiness. Sin is separation from God. We can't continue on the wrong path and draw closer to God. To draw near to Him, we must repent, make changes, and choose the right path.

Salvation restores our walk with God when we put our faith in Him. Salvation is a matter of faith. The strength of faith comes from the one in whom I put my faith. A strong faith misdirected to an unworthy target such as a religious leader, a government program, or my own ability has no saving power. On the other hand, as Jesus explains in Luke 17:6, faith as small as a mustard seed is powerful, provided it is faith in God. I may on occasion have weak faith and at other times strong faith, but the power of salvation is not altered, because my faith is in the unchanging power of God.

God readily and freely gives salvation. However, we all recognize that God's underlying design of the universe includes the built-in requirement that the books must balance. Scientists, for instance, speak of the law of conservation of energy. If energy is used in one place, it must come from some other place. Our own daily observation shows that nothing is truly free. A free meal requires that someone else pays for it. The free gift of salvation and forgiveness of sins must come from another source. That source is Jesus Christ.

Sins can be forgiven only if a sacrifice is made for those sins. God sent His Son, Jesus Christ, to die on the cross and provide for our salvation. "For God so loved the world that he gave his one and only Son, that whoever believes in him shall not perish but have eternal life" (John 3:16).

Because I have accepted salvation, I will emulate the life of Jesus. I will pray, read scripture, follow Jesus' example in baptism, join in fellowship with other believers, and share my joys and sorrows with them. I will strive to serve Jesus in every aspect of my life. But as I follow Jesus, I must remain humble and not think that I can justify my own salvation.

MAY CHRIST DWELL IN YOUR HEARTS

"In him and through faith in him we may approach God with freedom and confidence. I ask you, therefore, not to be discouraged because of my sufferings for you, which are your glory. For this reason I kneel before the Father, from whom his whole family in heaven and on earth derives its name. I pray that out of his glorious riches he may strengthen you with power through his Spirit in your inner being, so that Christ may dwell in your hearts through faith" (Ephesians 3:12–17).

SALVATION EMBRACED

Heavenly Father, I have made the decision to be born again. I have embraced Your salvation and turned my life over to You. My desire is to grow in knowledge of Your will. I want to reform my life to reflect Your love. I will face daily tests, but I know You won't allow Satan to overwhelm me. Please guide me to bring the good news of Your salvation to others.

PRAYER FOR SALVATION

If you confess with your mouth, "Jesus is Lord," and believe in your heart that God raised him from the dead, you will be saved.
ROMANS 10:9

Lord, I humbly bow before you now and confess my sins to you. I am sorry for all of my wrongdoing and I ask Your forgiveness. I believe Jesus is the Son of God and that He died on a cross and was raised from the dead. He conquered death so that I might really live—in power and purpose here on earth and forever with Him in heaven. I choose You. Please be my Savior and my Lord.

THANK YOU FOR SAVING ME

Thanks be to God for his indescribable gift!
2 CORINTHIANS 9:15

Lord, I thank You for my salvation. I thank You for Your indescribable gift of eternal life and the power to do Your will today. I can hardly fathom how You suffered, yet You did it all for me—for every person on this planet. Mocked and beaten, You bled for my sins. You had victory over death so we could live. You made a way for me and I am eternally grateful. Thank You, Lord.

A NEW BEGINNING

Lord, now that I am devoted to You heart and soul, I am a new creation. Thank You for washing away my old ways of thinking and behavior and for empowering me to live a new life. Your love changes me! Help me to live this new life with wisdom, making the right choices. Give me the courage to love the way You love. Teach me Your ways as we journey together on this path toward heaven. . .toward home.

GRACE ALONE

Lord, You give the best gifts! I receive the love gift of my salvation, knowing that it is by grace that I have been saved, through faith. I didn't do anything to deserve it or earn it. I know my works did not save me, for if they did then I could boast about it. Instead, You saved me by grace so I can now do good works—things You prepared in advance for me to do—to bring glory to Your name.

ONLY JESUS SAVES

Lord, Your Word says that salvation is found in no one else but God's Son, Jesus Christ. Only His name has the power to save. Our society likes to propose alternative ideas and try to convince me that I can find life in other ways—buying more things or finding romance or looking a certain way. Not true! I choose to believe in Jesus, not in other gods, not in other religious philosophies, not in materialism. Thank You for Your power to save.

RETURN TO YOUR FIRST LOVE

Lord, You know how prone I am to wander. So many ideas pull at my emotions every day—from the media to the people at work—trying to steer me in other directions and away from You. Forgive me for not putting You first. I am sorry. You are my first love. I don't want to forsake You; I want to follow You. Teach me the way of love as I learn to know You more.

POWER OF THE CROSS

For the message of the cross is foolishness to those who are perishing,
but to us who are being saved it is the power of God.
1 CORINTHIANS 1:18

Lord, I thank You for the wisdom to know the truth. People who do not know You think that the message of the cross—Jesus dying for the forgiveness of our sins—is foolishness. Truly, it is the power of God and it saves us. Your power is amazing; there is no one like You. No one else can bring the dead back to life, perform miracles, and change lives like mine. Please help other people to know the power of the cross, too.

GIFT OF THE HOLY SPIRIT

"You have made known to me the paths of life;
you will fill me with joy in your presence."
ACTS 2:28

Lord, I have repented of my sins and asked You to come into my life. I have received Your forgiveness. I thank You that Your Holy Spirit now lives inside me. What a gift! I choose to acknowledge this gift and ask that You would empower me to live a Spirit-filled life. Let my thoughts and actions be full of life and light and love, so others may see Christ in me.

ENERGIZED LIVING

Lord, I am truly amazed at Your great power. By the power of God Jesus was raised from the dead. And You will raise me, too. You lift my spirits from sadness to joy. You give me energy when my kids have depleted me. You help me find funds when my car needs repair. You give me friends to encourage me and share my life with. You heal bodies and broken relationships. Thank You for the power to live this life every day.

GOD'S PRESENCE

"The virgin will be with child and will give birth to a son, and they will call him Immanuel"—which means, "God with us."
MATTHEW 1:23

Lord, I thank You for sending Your Son, God with Us, Immanuel. Born of a virgin, You came to point us to the truth that saves us. You chose twelve disciples who followed You and learned the way to really live. You healed the sick; You gave sight to the blind. You were known for Your miracles and Your radical love for all kinds of people. Thank You for Your presence and that You live in me today.

RESTORED RELATIONSHIPS

A man is not justified by observing the law, but by faith in Jesus
Christ. So we, too, have put our faith in Christ Jesus that we may
be justified by faith in Christ and not by observing the law,
because by observing the law no one will be justified.
GALATIANS 2:16

Lord, You know how painful it is when things are not right
between friends. I long for connected relationships, where people
live in peace and harmony, and there is no resentment between
them. What a joy it is to know that I am made right with God by
faith. We can communicate freely, talking and listening, enjoying
each other as heart friends. I want to live in a growing love
relationship with You. Thank You for restoration and righteousness.

FORGIVEN

Lord, I am grateful for Your forgiveness. It's Your name, the name
of Jesus, that covers our sins when we believe in You. As I receive
Your pardon, empower me to have mercy on others. I thank You
that I am forgiven and free. Please help me to forgive others when
they've hurt me, knowing that You are the One who brings justice.
And please give me the power to forgive myself, too.

TO LOVE AND OBEY

Lord, I love You. And because of that I choose to obey You. Teach me Your ways as You make Your home in me. Clean out my cupboards of selfishness, and wash away the negative thoughts from my closets. Change my wrong ways of thinking—about myself and others—so I can be a vessel of hope and light. Help me to know You better. . .to be a doer of the Word, not just a hearer. . .to live what I believe.

NOT ASHAMED

Lord, I am not ashamed of the Gospel. Your words have the power to bring salvation to every person who believes. I don't want to hide the light of truth, but instead to let it shine from my life so others will see Christ in me. When people ask me about the source of my joy, give me the words to share so they can know You, too. Help me bring glory to You as I stand with courage and strength in the truth.

LET'S GROW

*Like newborn babies, crave pure spiritual milk,
so that by it you may grow up in your salvation.*
1 PETER 2:2

Lord, I want to grow up spiritually. I want to transition from a newborn baby who drinks only milk to a more mature believer who craves the "meat" of deeper things. I want to move from head knowledge to heart experience with You. I want to know what it means to enjoy Your presence, not just to make requests. Step-by-step and day-by-day, teach me to learn and follow Your ways.

I WILL FOLLOW YOU

*Then he said to them all: "If anyone would come after me,
he must deny himself and take up his cross daily and follow me.
For whoever wants to save his life will lose it, but whoever
loses his life for me will save it."*
LUKE 9:23–24

Lord, here I am before You. I am ready to "take up my cross" and follow You. Every day I want to be with You, empowered by You, and loved so deeply that I am changed. Show me what it means to lose my life in order to save it. Teach me about surrender, knowing You lift me up to do Your good purposes. Transform me, Lord. Teach me to follow You.

WORDS OF LIFE

Lord, You have the words of eternal life that allow us to cross over from death to life, from bondage to freedom, and from misery to peace. Words can be so hurtful at times, but Your words bring life, hope, and healing. You did not come to condemn me, but to save me and free me from death. Fill me with Your words of life and hope so I may use them to encourage others.

SEA OF FORGIVENESS

Lord, I see all sorts of discarded items in lakes that have been drained. Covered in slime, they are even more disgusting than when tossed away. The evil one wants me to dredge up those sins You have forgiven and forgotten. He wants me to live in the past. Lord, point me instead to the future. With You, I'm free to try again without the baggage of past failures holding me down.

MY STRESSES—
THE POWER OF REST AND REFRESHMENT

Stress is not a new problem. Remember Elijah? After an amazing victory on Mount Carmel, we find this prophet running for his life as fear replaced faith. First Kings 19 tells us that once he made his escape, Elijah rested beneath a broom tree where he "prayed that he might die. 'I have had enough, LORD,' he said. 'Take my life'" (v. 4). Then he lay down and fell asleep.

Have you ever felt like Elijah, saying, "Lord, I can't take it anymore," and then fallen into bed? But fortunately, as He did to Elijah, God is ready to minister to us in the midst of stress, to feed us and give us rest on every side, to fuel us with direction, compassion, and encouragement.

Now that we know where to go and whom to turn to, what can we do to protect ourselves against stress, to shore up our foundation of trust in God, so that our true color will be a consistent and overwhelming peace of Christ—within and without?

The first protective measure against stress is to make sure we take a weekly Sabbath rest. Each Sunday, worship with your fellow believers and then take the time to rest—really rest. Spend time in His presence, reading God's Word and Christian literature. Feed your mind as you rest your body. In your quiet time, give the Spirit a chance to light upon you, giving you discernment, realigning your priorities, and allowing you to see your life, circumstances, needs, and desires through the eyes of God.

Second, take a *daily* Sabbath rest, something our Lord did on a regular basis. Luke 5:16 says, "Jesus often withdrew to lonely places and prayed." Gordon MacDonald wrote, "True rest is happening when we pause regularly amidst daily routines to sort out the truths and commitments by which we are living." When you eagerly seek the Lord throughout the day, you will find Him and He will give you rest on every side (see 2 Chronicles 15:15).

Third, focus on and trust in God. In times of anxiety, we tend to let fear replace faith. We feel like Job: "What I feared has come upon me; what I dreaded has happened to me. I have no peace, no quietness; I have no rest, but only turmoil" (Job 3:25–26). Constantly remind yourself that with Jesus, you have nothing to fear. You can trust in the One who will never leave you nor forsake you. Continually shore up that trust by claiming God's promises, reading the Word, and applying it to your life. Keep your eye on Christ, not your fears or circumstances.

Fourth, daily ask God to help you keep your peace and give you joy on the journey through life, knowing that stress, although torturous at times, *can* make you a stronger person (see James 1:2–4). All the while keep in mind that no matter how difficult a situation may seem, nothing is impossible with God.

Finally, give your burdens to Jesus and leave them there. His shoulders were made to carry them. "Come to Me, all you who labor and are heavy laden, and I will give you rest" (Matthew 11:28 NKJV).

Continually turn to God, resting in His presence, trusting in Him, and allowing Him to carry your load. Build your life not on the world and its pleasures but on His words, hearing them and putting them into practice (see Matthew 7:24), and your foundation will be structurally sound, able to resist the cracks brought on by the storms of life.

OVERWHELMED

God, I have so many things to do today. I feel overwhelmed. But I am here to be Your hands and feet. You have known since the beginning of time what I am to accomplish each and every day. Give me the wisdom to do what You want me to do, to be the person You want me to be.

RENEW MY STRENGTH

I didn't get half the things I needed to do accomplished yesterday, Lord. And today I feel as if I have no energy. I am flagging, Lord, and I don't know what to do. So I arise early and come here to spend time with You. Calm my nerves. Remind me that the world is not going to fall apart if I don't accomplish everything on my to-do list today or even tomorrow, yet show me how to use my time wisely. Give my heart peace, and as I spend these moments with You, give me strength so that I may walk in Your power.

LET IT BE

I acknowledge that You are in control of everything, Lord, and that the things You want me to accomplish today will get done. I want to walk in Your will and not in mine. I want to lean on Your Word and take Your paths. I can only do that by putting my total trust in You as I go through this day. I want to be like Mary. I want to be Your servant, saying, "Let it be to me according to your word" (Luke 1:38 NKJV). So, Lord, help me to accomplish want You want me to do today, and let the rest be.

MY MAIN DESIRE

One thing I have desired of the LORD, that will I seek:
that I may dwell in the house of the LORD all the days of my life,
to behold the beauty of the LORD, and to inquire in His temple.
PSALM 27:4 NKJV

Lord, help me to keep the main thing the main thing—and that is to seek first the kingdom of God, beholding Your beauty, inquiring in Your temple. That is all that is truly important, not whether or not I get all my work done at home, the office, or church. As I receive requests for my time and ability, give me wisdom to say yes and no in accordance with Your will.

RUSH HOUR

Anxiety in the heart of man causes depression,
but a good word makes it glad.
PROVERBS 12:25 NKJV

Here I am, Lord, getting ready for another busy day, preparing myself to face rush hour. Help me to stay calm throughout this day and not get caught up in the frenzied pace of this world but to set a pace that is pleasing to You. Sure and steady wins the race, and my race is to win the prize of Your presence in my life. Help me to keep that in the forefront of my mind today. May I not become anxious but keep Your word of peace in my heart and be a beacon of peace in the presence of others.

CHANGE MY THOUGHTS

Lord, I don't want to be like the people of this world, running around at breakneck speed, trying to multitask until I'm so deep in the darkness I can no longer see the light of Your face. It's not all about doing; it's about being. Change *my* way of thinking to *Your* way of thinking. I take this to-do list and place it in Your capable hands. Help me to see this list through Your eyes. Show me clearly the steps I am to take today.

BEARING FRUIT

But his delight is in the law of the LORD, and in His law he
meditates day and night. He shall be like a tree planted by the
rivers of water, that brings forth its fruit in its season, whose leaf
also shall not wither; and whatever he does shall prosper.
PSALM 1:2–3 NKJV

I come to You this morning, meditating on Your law, Your Word.
That is my living water. You are the quencher of my thirst; You
provide everything for me. Because of Your presence in my life, I
can bring forth the fruit You want me to bear. As I go through the
activities of this day, may Your hand be upon me so that whatever
I do will prosper. To Your good and great glory, Lord, amen!

KEEPING PRIORITIES STRAIGHT

"God is with you in all that you do."
GENESIS 21:22 NKJV

Lord, as I go through this day, help me to keep my priorities
straight. It's not all about what I do but how I treat others. Show
me how to love those I come in contact with as I go through
my daily routine and run my errands. Help me be a person of
compassion. When people see me, I want them to recognize You,
because that's what the world needs more of these days—Your
love, Your face, Your presence, Your light.

CAPTURING THOUGHTS

God, it seems like I need a reminder every moment of the day
to listen to Your voice. I keep getting caught up in the world of
busyness, and that's not where You want me to be. Help me not to
be overwhelmed by the demands of this society but to be open to
Your voice. I want to hear You speak to me all throughout the day.
I want to do only what You want me to do each moment. Remind
me to take each thought captive to Christ so that I am not misled,
going somewhere or doing something that is not of You.

NO WORRIES

I'm not letting the worries of this day get me away from You,
Lord. I'll not go out into the world seeking gold—a temporary
blessing at best—but You and Your will. I seek first Your presence
as I come to You in prayer. I lay myself before You as Your willing
servant. May everything I do today leave Your fingerprints,
because that is why You created me. Help me to be a blessing to
all those I meet.

PEACE AMID INTERRUPTIONS

Here I am, Lord, ready to receive my marching orders for today. Arm me with faith, love, and hope. I am strong in You. I expect You to be with me all through the day. There is nothing that can frustrate me when I remain in Your presence. With every interruption, I am calm and accepting, because the prince of this world, the evil one, is unable to steal my peace and joy. For You, my Lord and Savior, have overcome this world! Hallelujah!

LEAD ME BY THE HAND

Here we go, Lord—another morning with a thousand things to do. Lead me by the hand, for I don't know which way to go. I have trouble with my priorities, Lord. The only thing I seem to be able to remember is that You are first in all things. So here I am, seeking You first. Plan my day as You see fit. Direct my steps to walk Your path. Life can get so complicated, Lord, so help me to keep it simple, remembering that You are working in me both to will and to do for Your pleasure.

REST FOR THE WEARY

Lord, I need rest. I am so tired and worn out. I pray that I will sleep well at night. I ask for more energy during the day, and a more vibrant spirit. Lighten my load so I can have a better balance among my work, my ministry, and my home life. Replenish me, Lord. As I unwind in spirit and body, please fill me with peace and rest.

GOOD EMOTIONAL HEALTH

Lord, I thank You for all the emotions we have. Help me to enjoy stable and good emotional health. I pray for wholeness in my feelings. I pray for more confidence, and that I would find my competence in You. I ask for healthier self-esteem—that I would know my true worth and value in who I am in Christ. I pray for more laughter, fun, and play in my life. Thank You for caring about all aspects of my health—my mind, my emotions, and my body.

HEALER OF HEARTS, BINDER OF WOUNDS

My heart is broken. I no longer have any strength. Fill me with Your power. Put Your arms around me. Let me linger in Your presence, bask in Your love. You are all I need. For without You, I can do nothing. Quench my thirst with Your living water. Feed me with Your bread of life. Nourish me deep within. I come to You in despair. I leave filled with joy.

GOD'S GLORY, NOT MINE

Whatever you do, do all to the glory of God.
1 CORINTHIANS 10:31 NASB

It's all for You, Lord, everything I do today. I refuse to get caught up in the mad rush. I refuse to seek only temporal satisfaction. I am here to please You and You only. Help me not to stretch myself so thin that I am unable to do the things You want me to do. I am here for You and for You alone. Give me the energy I need to accomplish those tasks for Your glory. And tonight may You say, "Ah, my good and faithful servant, well done!"

WITH HIM EACH MOMENT

Seek first God's kingdom and what God wants.
Then all your other needs will be met as well.
MATTHEW 6:33 NCV

I can't seem to find any time, Lord. It's always rush, rush, rush.
I need to remember that I am already with You in the heavens.
Calm my heart. Help me to breathe slower. I want to relax here
at Your feet. I want to smell Your perfume, touch Your robe, hear
Your voice. When I do Your work today, everything else will then
fall into place. I lean back against Your knees, waiting to hear
Your voice.

WITH ALL THAT IS WITHIN ME

Everything I am, all that is within me, I draw upon as I praise
Your holy name. You have done so many great things and have
given me the power to do even greater things as I allow You to
live through me. Thank You for healing me, for forgiving me. You
are an awesome God!

LIGHT IN MY DARKNESS

Lord, often I am afraid. In the dark, challenging times of my life, I can't always see the way. I don't know what to do or where to go. But You are light! I thank You that You can see in the dark—the darkness is as light to You—so I don't have to be afraid. When my enemies try to ruin my life, they don't stand a chance, Lord. You save me. No matter what happens, I will be confident in You.

GOD'S POWER TO CONQUER FEAR

Lord, You never give in to defeat. You are a strong conqueror of sin and evil. I need Your authority and influence to muscle fear out of my life. You called Moses to lead the Israelites from slavery to freedom. Lead me from my own personal bondage to walk in freedom and peace. Show Your power in my life and let Your name be lifted up. You get the credit, Lord—let everyone know what You have done to change me.

MY TIME—THE POWER OF PRIORITIES

It's important to be purposeful with your time. Every person on the planet has the same amount of time each day. You have to learn to manage yourself, because time refuses to be managed. (*Time* management is really *self*-management—learning to use the inflexible twenty-four hours of the day in ways that best help you accomplish your goals.)

No one can change time, so you must continually remain aware of it. There are tools available to help you be more conscious of your time: clocks, watches, calendars, personal organizers, seminars, and computer programs. And still, we often find it difficult to make time to do everything we have to do.

Think of time as a currency—where do you spend it? Who or what will you give your time to today? Is that time wisely invested? You can probably think of many occasions when you let time get away from you. We've all looked up from a project or activity and realized we'd spent much more time on what we were doing than we intended.

Jesus said, "Wherever your treasure is, there the desires of your heart will also be" (Matthew 6:21 NLT). So how and where you choose to spend your time says a lot about what is most important to you.

The key to successful self-management is in setting priorities. Think back over the past few days or months. How did you spend your time, effort, and energy? Did you have a goal you were pushing to reach?

We need to allocate our time based on what we believe to be most important. Are our friends and family important? Then we schedule time for them. We *invest* our time in them.

As we read the Bible, it becomes clear that we are God's greatest priority. He has spent much of His time focused on bringing us back into relationship with Him.

Your relationship with God is the foundation of your success in everything else you do. All you will ever need is found in your relationship with Him. As you grow in Him, you become strong, healthy, and full of His love, and then you are able to overflow into the lives of others.

Through prayer and commitment to your relationship with God, He can help you make every minute count. He can help you focus on the things that are most important to you and to Him.

THE FIRST PRIORITY

Father, You are my everything! Without You, I wouldn't even be here. Forgive me for allowing so many other things to squeeze between me and You. Help me to become more diligent in my time with You. It fills me with the strength I need to make it day after day. I love You so much! I never want to take our relationship for granted.

"Love the Lord your God with all your heart and with all your soul and with all your mind.' This is the first and greatest commandment."
MATTHEW 22:37–38

MAKING PRAYER A PRIORITY

God, I am reaching out to You from the deepest places in my heart. I love You and want to make prayer a favorite part of my day. Help me to be consistent in spending time with You. Teach me to recognize and reject the distractions and the unending list of things that keep me too busy for You. My relationship with You is my highest priority and strongest commitment. Remind me of that and give me the determination to spend time in prayer no matter what situations arise. Let nothing keep me from You!

QUIET WATERS

He makes me lie down in green pastures,
he leads me beside quiet waters.
PSALM 23:2

My Shepherd, my Lord, my Savior, lead me beside the still waters. Lie with me in the green pastures. Restore my soul. Lead my down the paths of *Your* choosing today. With You by my side, I fear no evil. You are my Comfort and my Guide. I am happy in Your presence. Your goodness and Your mercy are with me this minute, this hour, and this day. Thank You, Lord, for leading me here and making me whole—for being the Shepherd of my life.

MORNING MEDITATION

Give heed to the voice of my cry, my King and my God,
for to You I will pray. My voice You shall hear in the morning,
O LORD; in the morning I will direct it to You, and I will
look up. . . . Make Your way straight before my face.
PSALM 5:2–3, 8 NKJV

You defend me, You love me, You lead me. How great is that! How great are You! Too wonderful for words. This morning in Your presence, I rejoice. This morning, I direct my prayers to You, knowing that You will hear my words and interpret my groans. I am directing my voice to You, Lord, and patiently await Your instructions.

DAILY CHORES

Lord, my job can become a steady pounding of dreary, mundane tasks. They can seem to have no consequence or importance. Renew my passion for my daily responsibilities. I know You didn't create me to live a life of mediocrity but of excellence. Keep me from settling for second best. May Your presence be with me in the workplace. Let me be happy at my work and with what my work can bring to my family.

JESUS COMPLETES HIS WORK

"Father, the time has come. Glorify your Son, that your Son may glorify you. For you granted him authority over all people that he might give eternal life to all those you have given him. Now this is eternal life: that they may know you, the only true God, and Jesus Christ, whom you have sent. I have brought you glory on earth by completing the work you gave me to do" (John 17:1–4).

LIVING IN THE NOW

I can't change the past, but I think about it a lot. It's a waste of time, and I hate for my mind to go there. I don't want to recount my past mistakes—I've been forgiven. Lord, help me to focus on today. Help me to keep my attention on the priorities You have given me. Help me to live in the present. Show me what I can do today to make an eternal difference.

> *"And the second [greatest commandment] is like it:*
> *'Love your neighbor as yourself.'"*
> MATTHEW 22:39

EVERY MINUTE COUNTS

What I do today affects my tomorrow. Lord, help me to be conscious of time-wasters. I don't want to be idle and lazy. Show me Your plan and the things I need to put my hands to, but at the same time help me to balance my life so I take good care of my body and mind with the right amount of rest. As I walk with You, I know I am pursuing the things You want me to do. I ask You to help me be in the right place at the right time every time.

WHEN I'M OVERCOMMITTED

God, I did it again—I'm overcommitted, stressed, and overwhelmed. Someone I made a promise to is going to be disappointed in me. Why can't I just say no to start with? Help me to manage better and be realistic about what I can accomplish in one day. Give me wisdom when others ask me to help them. It's better to say no and help later, if I can, than to make a promise and then let someone down who was counting on me. When I make promises, help me to have the integrity to keep them.

SACRIFICES

I only have so much time every day. Lord, help me to spend my time wisely, on the things that matter most. Day-to-day things are continually in my face, screaming for my attention, but there are also things that are eternal, like people. Help me realize my time spent for eternal things, like spending time with others, is not a sacrifice, but a reward.

WHEN OTHERS FAIL ME

When others fail me, it makes me feel unimportant to them.
It hurts my feelings and I want to be angry. Remind me of the
times when circumstances were out of my control and I missed
a commitment and failed someone. Fill me with compassion
and understanding for their situation. Help me to get over it and
show them Your love.

> *Make allowance for each other's faults,*
> *and forgive anyone who offends you. Remember,*
> *the Lord forgave you, so you must forgive others.*
> COLOSSIANS 3:13 NLT

WHEN I MAKE EXCUSES

God, I know You aren't about excuses, but I make them when
I don't want to do something I need to do. Forgive me for not
being diligent. Give me strength to tackle the difficult tasks first,
even those things I find boring. Help me to do the things I don't
want to do as if I were doing them for You. That would give the
job more purpose, at least for me. And remind me never to leave
a job unfinished that I've committed to do. I want to leave a good
impression on others, especially when I'm representing You.

WHEN I'M DISTRACTED

Lord, my mind is wandering again. Help me to stay focused on what I have in front of me. I have the mind of Christ, and I am determined to stay steady until I've finished the task. I will not look to the right or the left. I refuse to be distracted. I push my worries to the side. I will accomplish what I've set my heart to do. I will not quit. I have a mission and I will achieve it.

GETTING THE MOST OUT OF MY DAY

Father, when I was a child, a day seemed so long that sometimes I got bored. Now I find there are not enough hours to complete what I need to do each day. I need Your wisdom about how to budget my time. Show me how I can use it more efficiently.

ENJOYING TIME ALONE

God, sometimes I feel guilty when I make time to be alone. My relationships are important to me, but time alone is important, too. Jesus took time to get away and be alone. Teach me to follow His example. Remind me to spend that time reflecting on the many good things You have done in my life. Remembering those times helps me to grow stronger in my faith. Time alone is a great opportunity to study Your Word and let You minister to me. Help me to enjoy my alone time with You.

TOOLS FOR TIME

Lord, help me to find tools to make me more effective in the use of my time. Bring the right people across my path to educate me about how to use the tools that best fit my personality and gifts.

KNOWING WHAT'S IMPORTANT

Father, help me to know what is most important. I know that growing in my relationship with You is first, so I need Your help in staying true to that commitment. Second, I need Your help in valuing the relationships You bring into my life and caring for them with the power of Your love. Please tap me on the shoulder and remind me when I'm becoming too busy. I don't want to miss the most important priorities in life.

THE RIGHT TIME

Father, I have lots of ideas. There's so much I want to do, but I just don't know when to do it. Your timing is everything. You have ordered my steps and You know the way that I should go. I ask the Holy Spirit to lead and guide me. Give me assurance and peace to know when it's time to step forward. Thank You for making everything happen in Your time, not mine.

OVEREXTENDED

Lord, I had a friend who overextended himself in an attempt to have it all. Then at a fund-raising dinner, he collapsed. Stress, the killer of men in their middle years, had almost taken its toll. Father, help me give balance to my life. May my drive at work never jeopardize my health, alienate my family, distance my friends, or detract from my service to You.

EVERYTHING COMES FROM GOD

"Wealth and honor come from you; you are the ruler of all things. In your hands are strength and power to exalt and give strength to all. Now, our God, we give you thanks, and praise your glorious name. But who am I, and who are my people, that we should be able to give as generously as this? Everything comes from you, and we have given you only what comes from your hand" (1 Chronicles 29:12–14).

MY WORK—THE POWER OF A JOB WELL DONE

God the Potter has created each of us for a specific purpose and continually shapes us as it seems good to Him (see Jeremiah 18:4). For what has God fashioned you? If you're not sure, pray for guidance, with a mind open enough to accept whatever the Lord tells you. God will give you courage, gifts, and opportunities, as well as combine your experience, talents, and knowledge, in order to place you where He needs you. Each day tap into the power of commitment, keeping your course steady so that you will be amply rewarded, now and at the end of your journey, as a "good and faithful servant" (Matthew 25:23).

Don't let the daily grind of routine crush your spirit. "A man can do nothing better than to. . .find satisfaction in his work. This too, I see, is from the hand of God, for without him, who can eat or find enjoyment?" (Ecclesiastes 2:24–25). So whether your job is performing repetitive household chores, continually running the widget-making machine, driving the school bus along its daily route, or teaching the same old lesson plan year after year, find joy in the journey. Don't let the monotony of life get you down, but keep *God* first in your life, "for the kingdom of God is. . . righteousness, peace and joy in the Holy Spirit" (Romans 14:17).

Don't become so immersed in your present job that you miss the opportunities God puts in your path. Because God gives you both the means and the desire to fulfill your purpose for Him, He may prompt you to take some evening courses, invest in a hobby, or change jobs. All of these stepping-stones may be training for future endeavors. If you're too involved in your current job, you may miss His promptings.

Finally, don't work just for the money, for a man "cannot serve both God and money" (Matthew 6:24 NLT). Frederick Buechner wrote, "If [a man's] in it only for the money, the money is all he gains, and when he finally retires, he may well ask himself if it was worth giving most of his life for." We must beware of having our eyes on the wrong treasure to the detriment of our souls. Jesus said, "You say, 'I am rich. I have everything I want. I don't need a thing!' And you don't realize that you are wretched and miserable and poor and blind and naked" (Revelation 3:17 NLT). Put your heart and soul into whatever you set your hand to, doing it to serve others and God, not mammon.

Daily commit your work to God and consistently seek His direction. Remember that He continually opens doors for His children (see 1 Corinthians 16:9; 2 Corinthians 2:12; and Colossians 4:3). But you have to keep your ears open to His voice and your eyes open to opportunity. Through all your life's work, consistently ask Christ for His advice and direction, remembering that all works committed to God will be supported by God.

THANK YOU FOR MY WORK

Lord, I praise You and thank You for my work. You are full of goodness and grace. My occupation gives me the ability to shape lives and influence people in positive ways every day, whether it's taking time for teachable moments with my kids or being a listening ear for a coworker. Thank You for my job and the ability to be a "missionary" wherever my feet tread. Season my words so that others may taste and see that my Lord is good.

GOD'S WILL FOR MY WORK LIFE

Lord, I need wisdom and guidance in my work life. Please show me if this is the vocation I should be in right now or if I should change and find another job. I want to use my skills and abilities, as well as my interests, for Your glory. When I feel underutilized and yearn for something more, reveal to me where I can best serve in the coming season of my life.

GUIDED BY THE HOLY SPIRIT

I understand, Lord, that the Holy Spirit is just waiting to lead me. Open my mind and heart and ears to His voice today. Still the constant chatter in my head that keeps reminding me of all the tasks I need to get done today. Give me the plan You have already laid out for my life. Shape me into the person You want me to be so that I can do what You have created me to do. Lead me step-by-step, Lord. I commit my way and my plans to Your purpose.

MY PURPOSE

Lord, what am I supposed to do? I'm not sure why I'm at this job. Or am I not to have a career but be a stay-at-home parent? Have I made the wrong decision? Am I walking in Your will, or have I been led by my own desires? Show me, Lord, which way You want me to go. If there is some new challenge You want me to undertake, please tell me. Let me hear Your voice. Renew my mind this morning so that I can know Your good and perfect will for my life.

SPIRIT-FILLED

*I have filled him with the Spirit of God, giving him
great wisdom, ability, and expertise in all kinds of crafts.*
EXODUS 31:3 NLT

You have filled me with Your Spirit. I have been given wisdom,
understanding, education, and talent for many lines of work.
Show me how I can use my knowledge, understanding, and
abilities to do the work You have set out for me. Show me the
paths You want me to take. What do You want me to do with my
hands, my life, my gifts? They all come from You, the One I want
to serve.

A NEW MIND

*Let God transform you into a new person by changing
the way you think. Then you will learn to know God's
will for you, which is good and pleasing and perfect.*
ROMANS 12:2 NLT

I'm so confused, Lord. I seem to have the wrong mind-set today.
Instead of looking to Your leading, I seem to be focused in on the
worldly aspects of life. And I know that's not where You want
my thoughts to be. Give me the mind of Christ. Make my needs
simple. Change my life, my thoughts, my desires. I want to live a
life that is good, perfect, and pleasing to You.

WORKING WITH EXCELLENCE

Lord, You give me work to do every day. Whether it's at home or in the marketplace, help me to honor You in my efforts. I don't want to be satisfied with mediocrity. I ask that You would empower me to do superior work and bring glory to Your name. Help me not to be a clock-watcher or time-waster, but to find fulfillment in the tasks before me. Help me to be a person of excellence, integrity, and good ideas in my place of employment.

GETTING ALONG WITH COWORKERS

Lord, I thank You for the people with whom I work, those I spend time with every day. Help us to nurture an environment of peace and harmony. When people get along, it's a good thing! Give us respect for one another, and patience to deal with disagreements. Even though we're all busy, help us to have more connectedness and unity—so we can be more efficient and find more enjoyment in our work. Lord, please bless me and my relationships in the workplace.

RESPONDING WELL TO CRITICISM

*A fool shows his annoyance at once, but a prudent man
overlooks an insult. A truthful witness gives honest testimony,
but a false witness tells lies. Reckless words pierce like a sword,
but the tongue of the wise brings healing.*
PROVERBS 12:16–18

Lord, I don't like being criticized. I ask for a calm spirit when
others make cutting remarks. Please give me insight to know if
what is said is true—and if I need to make changes in my life.
If not, Lord, I ask You to heal my heart from these verbal barbs.
Please give me patience and discernment to keep my cool and
not lash out in retaliation. Please bring our relationship through
this criticism.

BLESSINGS FROM THE WORK OF YOUR HANDS

*The LORD your God will bless you in all your harvest and in
all the work of your hands, and your joy will be complete.*
DEUTERONOMY 16:15

Lord, I ask that You would bless the work of my hands. As I sit
at a computer, or fold laundry, or teach a classroom of children,
may my work be meaningful and bear good fruit. I pray for a
spirit of joy during the day as I go about my business. I pray for a
cheerful countenance and a willing, servant's heart. I dedicate my
work life to You, Lord, for Your good purposes and blessings.

A PLACE FOR MY GIFTS

Lord, I'm not currently using the gifts I believe You gave me. Help me find a place where I can use my talents, experience, and knowledge to Your good. And while I am in my current position, help me to do my work for Your glory, because You are the manager of my life. Give me Your peace, joy, and direction. I so desperately need to spend these moments in Your presence to prepare my spirit for the tasks of this day. Do not leave me, Lord. Stay in my heart now and forever.

WORKING TO HIS HONOR

Everything I do and everything I have is for Your honor and Your glory—not mine! I am the ambassador of Your one and only Son, Jesus Christ. Give me that attitude today, so that everyone who looks at me, hears me, and speaks to me will see His face and feel His presence. I want to become less so that He can become more. I am Your servant, Lord—help me to serve productively and creatively. All, Lord, to Your honor!

GREAT EXPECTATIONS

Lord, I want to be like David, serving my own generation by Your will. No matter how small the job or role, fill me with great expectations that You are going to do a powerful work through me. I ask this not for my glory, but to demonstrate to others the power of living in You. Imbue me with hope and thanksgiving. I do not know the entire plan You have for my life. Help me not to look too far ahead and thus miss the joy of day-to-day living. Thank You for hearing this prayer.

HIS WORK PLAN

My goal is to live the life You have planned for me. Keep me on the road to Your will. Show me the ways You want me to go. Help me avoid the worldly traps of money, discontentment, grief, envy, workaholism, and tedium. Keep me close to Your side and consistently in Your presence, ever open to hearing Your voice. Give me the power to live Your plan for me. Thank You for all You are doing in my life!

THE RIGHT ATTITUDE

Do everything without complaining and arguing.
PHILIPPIANS 2:14 NLT

I'm getting tired of my job and my boss, Lord. It seems like the same thing day in and day out. I know I should be grateful for the work I have been given, but I can't seem to get past this wall of negativity. Give me the right mind-set, Lord, before I even go into work. And then help me remember that I am working for You. Give me the mind and servant attitude of Christ this morning and help me maintain it throughout this day.

JOYFUL SERVANT

"Well done, my good and faithful servant. You have been faithful in handling this small amount, so now I will give you many more responsibilities. Let's celebrate together!"
MATTHEW 25:23 NLT

I want to be a good and faithful servant sharing Your joy, but I feel like the world is bringing me down. That and my job. Help me to be faithful in what You have given me, and then, if it is Your will, put more things in my care. I want to feel and share the joy that working for and with You brings. Help me to renew my mind this morning, because my head is definitely in the wrong place. Touch me with Your compassion and grace. Fill me with Your Spirit, Your joy, Your love.

REDUCING STRESS

*Do not be anxious about anything, but in everything, by prayer
and petition, with thanksgiving, present your requests to God.*
PHILIPPIANS 4:6

Lord, I have so much to do—please help me! Deadlines and
details swirl around me like a swarm of bees. I feel heavy pressure
with my heavy workload. Help me to do what needs to be done
each day, so I can stop worrying and rest well at night. I give You
my anxiety and stress—I release it all to You, Lord. As Your peace
covers me, the peace that passes all understanding, may it guard my
heart and mind in Christ Jesus. I rest in the comfort of Your love.

BALANCING WORK AND LIFE

*Am I now trying to win the approval of men, or of God?
Or am I trying to please men? If I were still trying to
please men, I would not be a servant of Christ.*
GALATIANS 1:10

Lord, every day is a juggling act with work, my home, my spouse,
kids, ministry, and friends. I rarely have time for myself—just to
be with You, or even to remember who I am. Teach me to center
on You, Lord, and keep my focus. I can't please everyone, and
really, You've never asked me to. You are the One I seek to please.
Be the hub of my heart, the steady center that moves the wheel
of my life forward.

SERVANT-STYLE LEADERSHIP

Lord, teach me to be a leader by being a servant. Your ways are so unlike the ways of the world. Strange as it may seem, You say that "whoever wants to become great among you must be your servant." Help me to be more like Christ, as He did not come to be served, but to serve. Remove pride, selfishness, and arrogance from my life—and supply me, Lord, with humility and a heart that serves.

WHO'S THE BOSS?

In God I trust; I will not be afraid. What can man do to me? I am under vows to you, O God; I will present my thank offerings to you.
Psalm 56:11–12

Lord, I pray for a right mind-set with the person for whom I work. Help me to submit to her authority and work with honesty and integrity. Yet, while I report to someone in my occupation, may I have the firm conviction that You are my highest authority. My ultimate trust is in You, Lord, not in any man or woman. As I report to You each day for guidance, help me to serve You well.

BE CONTENT

*I am not saying this because I am in need, for I have learned
to be content whatever the circumstances. I know what it is to
be in need, and I know what it is to have plenty. I have learned
the secret of being content in any and every situation, whether
well fed or hungry, whether living in plenty or in want.*
PHILIPPIANS 4:11–12

Lord, I often think about what could be and dream of a better
future. Sometimes, though, my thoughts are locked in the past,
stuck in disappointment and regret. Please help me to be content
with today, to live in this moment, no matter what my current
circumstances. In every situation, may I look to You for peace.
Still the storms in my heart, so whether I am at rest or in motion,
I can find Your serenity and strength.

A GOOD ATTITUDE

Lord, I lift up to You my attitude at work. As I go about my day,
may I have a positive outlook and a helpful spirit. Help me to
be encouraging and supportive to others. Amid the activity—
and sometimes the chaos—may my heart be at peace as the
Holy Spirit strengthens and empowers me. Be the Lord of my
emotions as I seek to serve You in my vocation.

FINDING MEANING AND PURPOSE

Lord, I thank You for the promise that You will fulfill Your purpose for me. Your love endures forever—You will not abandon the work of Your hands. Help me to put my hand to my tasks each day with a sense of meaning and purpose. Enlighten me to use my skills, abilities, and talents in life-changing ways—no matter how small or insignificant my work may seem at the moment. You see the bigger picture, Lord; You use everything for the good and for Your glory, even when I don't understand. Thank You, Lord.

FINDING SUCCESS

Commit to the LORD whatever you do,
and your plans will succeed.
PROVERBS 16:3

Lord, I ask for success and favor for all I put my hands to today. Bless my work, please. May the time and effort I put into it bear abundant fruit. I commit my plans to You, Lord, and surrender my will for Yours. In all I seek to accomplish, in all I hope to become as a woman of God, may my plans succeed. I pray for victory and triumph as You reveal to me what true success should look like in my life.

MY WORLD—THE POWER OF COMPASSION

Compassion is defined by *Merriam-Webster's Dictionary* as "sympathetic consciousness of others' distress together with a desire to alleviate it." Our God is the Father of compassion. He had so much sympathy for our suffering that He sent His one and only Son to die for us (see John 3:16). Do you share God's compassion? Do you realize that Jesus Christ wants to express through you what the Father expressed through Him, bringing love and hope to a hurting world? We, God's people, are to be clothed with compassion (see Colossians 3:12). What are you wearing today?

Some of us, when our tender hearts see the troubles of others, may think we are too far away or too powerless to help. But that is an untruth. Our prayers are full of heavenly power. They transcend time and space. We can be on our knees in our living rooms and reach a president in the White House, a homeless man on a city street, children starving in North Korea, missionaries in South America, or an AIDS worker in Africa. With the power of compassion combined with prayer, *we can make a difference*!

Nehemiah was an unselfish man of prayer who looked beyond himself and his needs. His example shows us what we need to do to be powerful intercessors for this world. Like Nehemiah, we need to find out what is happening outside the sphere of me, myself, and I. When Nehemiah met Hanani, one of his brothers who had come from Judah, Nehemiah *asked for news* of the Jews in Jerusalem. It was then that he found out the specifics of the remnant's desperate situation, how the wall of

Jerusalem was broken down, leaving the Jews defenseless against their enemies (see Nehemiah 1:1–3).

As soon as he heard of their situation, Nehemiah sat down and wept. He *felt compassion* and his heart mourned. The Bible says he fasted and *prayed*, asking God to hear him, remember His promises to His people, and give him success (see Nehemiah 1:4–11).

A few months later Nehemiah took wine to King Artaxerxes, and with one look at his cupbearer's face, which revealed "sadness of heart," the king inquired as to Nehemiah's troubles, asking what he could do for him. Here Nehemiah *took direct action* as he reached out to another. Through that assistance, he was able to personally assess the situation in Jerusalem and, ultimately, to help rebuild the wall.

When you hear of distress in the world and your heart responds with compassion, make a difference! Get down on your knees and pray with persistence. And if so led, take direct action. Be filled with confidence that God will work in the situation.

In this world, Jesus says we will have trouble. When things seem hopeless, we must be confident that Christ will meet us in the fire, as He did Shadrach, Meshach, and Abednego. When terror seems to reign on every side, continue faithfully onward, remembering that "if we are thrown into the blazing furnace, the God we serve is able to save us from it, and he will rescue us" (Daniel 3:17). Because of His unfailing compassion, we will not be consumed (see Lamentations 3:22).

PERSEVERANCE IN PRAYER

I feel like I've been praying forever for a situation that does not seem to be changing, Lord. I feel like Job: here I am on my knees in prayer while the entire world dissolves around me. But I know that You are in control. You know all things. So once again, I lift up my concern to You, confident that You will handle the situation in Your timing.

GOD'S HAND GUARDING US

Lord, sometimes I feel like Captain Kirk. When faced with the evils of this world, I want to say, "Beam me up, God!" But I know that no matter what happens in this world, Your hand is guarding us. And armed with Your compassion, we have the power to intercede for the hungry, the oppressed, the imprisoned, the homeless, the wounded.

REIGNING PEACE

"These things I have spoken to you, that in Me you may
have peace. In the world you will have tribulation;
but be of good cheer, I have overcome the world."
JOHN 16:33 NKJV

Dear God, how I pray for peace around the world. Some say
it's impossible—but with You all things are possible. And while
peace may not yet reign throughout the earth, with You in my
heart, peace reigns within, for you have overcome the world! May
all people feel Your peace within!

WISDOM AND UNDERSTANDING

Lord, I pray for insight into the people I serve. Give me
understanding as to their needs, so I can better relate to them
and be able to address their concerns. Help me to take an interest
in their particular culture, whether ethnic- or age-related. I pray
for wisdom on how to reach them, teach them, and bless them.

RELEASE MORE POWER IN MY MINISTRY

Lord God, I need You. I ask that You would release more of Your power into my life and ministry. God of peace, equip me with everything good to do Your will. Help me to have compassion, integrity, and wise leadership. Work in me what is pleasing to You, Lord. Empower me, enlighten me, and change me, so I can be more effective in serving. Let Your name be glorified and honored in all of my ministry activities.

COMPASSION FOR THE HUNGRY

Is there any encouragement from belonging to Christ?
Any comfort from his love? Any fellowship together in the Spirit?
Are your hearts tender and compassionate? Then make me truly
happy by agreeing wholeheartedly with each other, loving one another,
and working together with one mind and purpose.
PHILIPPIANS 2:1–2 NLT

With the compassion You show to us, Your abiding tenderness through thick and thin, today I reach out to the hungry here and abroad. Open up my eyes to how I can help. Show me where my hands can be used to help feed those who are starving. I want to serve others in the name of Jesus Christ, for that is what You have called us to do. Open a door for me. Show me what I can do to make this world a better place.

A HEART TO SERVE

The LORD is gracious and compassionate,
slow to anger and rich in love.
PSALM 145:8

Lord, I pray for a spirit of compassion. Help me to care about the needs of others and have genuine love for the ones I serve. Pour into me Your caring, kind Spirit, so I can be a blessing and minister out of a full heart. Fill me to overflowing so my ministry will be effective, growing, and blessed. May I walk in Your graciousness with a heart to serve.

PROVISION AND RESOURCES

The next day we landed at Sidon; and Julius, in kindness to Paul,
allowed him to go to his friends so they might provide for his needs.
ACTS 27:3

Lord, Your resources are unlimited. You delight to give Your children good gifts, to meet their needs. I boldly and humbly ask that You would provide for the needs of my ministry. Bring our ministry to the minds of people who are willing to give out of their God-given resources. May they give of their time, money, talents, or other resources to bless these ministry efforts to further Your kingdom.

FOR THE POOR AND NEEDY

"When you give to the needy, do not let your left hand know what your right hand is doing, so that your giving may be in secret. Then your Father, who sees what is done in secret, will reward you."
MATTHEW 6:3–4

Lord, I pray today for the poor and needy. Many need money, while others are poor in spirit. Please provide food and water to meet their physical needs and the Gospel of Jesus Christ and His saving love to fill their souls. Lord, show me how I can be part of the solution. Show me where I can give and serve. Use my abilities and finances to help, for Your glory.

FOR THOSE IN PRISON

"I was in prison and you came to visit me."
MATTHEW 25:36

Lord, I pray for the men and women in prison all over our country today. I ask for a revival—that many would come to know You, love You, and serve You. Help those who are incarcerated to know that You are the One who sets people free from the bondage of sin and wrongdoing. Help them to know that only You offer a life of hope and peace. In the darkness, help them to find Christ's forgiveness, joy, and light. Remind my heart, Lord, to visit those in prison and fulfill Your commands.

MISSION FIELD

Jesus, teach me, lead me, and send me. I realize the mission field is right outside my front door. My desire is to open the doors of opportunity as I find them in my community. Whether I plant, water, or harvest, my desire is to be a useful servant for You. Show me what needs to be done, and strengthen my resolve to do Your will enthusiastically.

FOR THOSE IN GRIEF

"Blessed are those who mourn, for they will be comforted."
MATTHEW 5:4

Lord, my friend has deep pain in her soul. I ask that You would comfort her. Be near, Lord; be near. May she rest in the strong and loving arms of the One who loves her most. Heal her heartache; heal her sorrow. You are One acquainted with grief, so You know her pain. Help her to know that You can relate, and that You care. One day soon, may she find healing and wholeness again.

FOR THE SICK

Is any one of you sick? He should call the elders of the church to pray over him and anoint him with oil in the name of the Lord. And the prayer offered in faith will make the sick person well; the Lord will raise him up. If he has sinned, he will be forgiven. Therefore confess your sins to each other and pray for each other so that you may be healed. The prayer of a righteous man is powerful and effective.
JAMES 5:14–16

Lord, I am praying for a person who is sick right now. She needs your healing touch on her body and her emotions. Heal her pain, Lord. Help her to sense Your presence, to know You are near. Be her comfort. I ask that she would not be afraid or lonely. I pray in faith, in the name and power of Jesus, for You to heal my friend. I ask that You would make her well.

WORKING TOGETHER

Lord, I pray the Holy Spirit will lead me in the service You want me to do. As I become a more active Christian, I will have greater contact with other Christians. We may not have exactly the same goals or approaches. We may not pursue our tasks with the same intensity. Should we disagree, help me put on the filter of love to work peacefully with others for Your glory.

COMMUNITY PEACE AND UNDERSTANDING

God, through the divine power of Your Spirit and Your Word, I pray for my neighborhood. Demolish the stronghold of evil within this community. Touch each heart with Your peace and understanding. You know what each family needs. Help me to be an encouragement to them. Be with me as I take a prayer walk around this neighborhood, lifting each family up to Your heavenly throne.

COMFORT FOR THE SUFFERING

Dearest Christ, I pray for Your bright, shining light to spread out into the world. For Your love to reach the ends of the earth. Give comfort to those who suffer from abuse and violence. Touch them with Your healing light and guard them with Your protective hand. Give them assurance that You are there. Allow them to feel Your presence, hear Your voice, feel Your touch.

CHANGE THE HEARTS OF TERRORISTS

Finally, all of you, live in harmony with one another;
be sympathetic, love as brothers, be compassionate and humble.
1 PETER 3:8

Dear Lord, please soften the calloused hearts of those who deem themselves terrorists. Exchange their hearts of stone for ones tender with love. Protect the innocent here and abroad, especially missionaries who risk their lives to spread Your light. Comfort those who have lost loved ones through the violence around the world.

VICTORY FOR YOUTH

For our struggle is not against flesh and blood, but against the rulers,
against the powers, against the world forces of this darkness, against
the spiritual forces of wickedness in the heavenly places.
EPHESIANS 6:12 NASB

Lord, I pray that You would oust the unseen evils from this land, that Your angels would battle fiercely against the dark forces corrupting our youth. Empower our youth leaders to claim a victory for young hearts. Show me how I can help at my church, how I can lead teens to You. Give parents the right words to say when dealing with their children.

PROTECTION FOR MISSIONARIES AND PASTORS

I pray for others with the confidence that You, dear Lord, hear my prayer. That although at times this world seems so unsettled, Your hand is upon our missionaries and pastors, guarding them when they are awake and as they sleep. Give them the strength to do what You have called them to do. Give them the means to help the lost, starving, diseased, and imprisoned. Give them wisdom as they reveal Your Word and reach into the darkness to spread Your light.

MESSAGE OF ETERNAL LIFE

The world may pass away, but Your love never fails. Those who believe in You will live with You forever. What a blessed thing! I pray that others around the world will hear the message so that they, too, can accept Your gift of eternal life. Show me how I can help spread the message, all to Your glory.

CLOTHED WITH COMPASSION

As I get down on my knees, I wrap myself within the cloak of compassion. I bring to You specific concerns for which You have led me to pray, knowing that You hear my prayer, confident that You will answer. And as I rise from the place of prayer, may Your kindness, humility, gentleness, and patience shine through me and lighten the hearts of others. I want to be Your servant. Help me to change the world.

HOME, SCHOOL, AND STREETS

Lord, there are so many dark forces within our schools, on the streets, and even in our homes. I pray for Your light to eliminate the evil among us. I know that no matter what, You will prevail, dear Jesus. You have overcome this world. You have the power to do the impossible. Show me how I can make this world a better place. Give me the heart to intercede for others and the courage to step in when and where I am needed.